"I Won't Be a Slave!"

I dedicate this book to my family
with gratitude and love

Cover design by Martin Best of My6productions, Toronto, Canada

I Won't Be a Slave!"

Selected Articles on Finnish Canadian Women's History

By

Varpu Lindström

ASPASIA BOOKS
Beaverton Ontario Canada

"I Won't Be a Slave!"
Selected Articles on Finnish Canadian Women's History
by Varpu Lindström
ISBN 978-0-9783488-8-5

Published in 2010 by
Aspasia Books, Inc.
25040 Maple Beach Road, R.R.1
Beaverton, ON L0K 1A0, Canada
aspasia@aspasiabooks.com
www.aspasiabooks.com

Library and Archives Canada Cataloguing in Publication
Lindström, Varpu, 1948-
"I won't be a slave!": selected articles on Finnish Canadian women's history / Varpu Lindström.

Includes bibliographical references.
ISBN 978-0-9783488-8-5

1. Finns--Canada--History--20th century. 2. Finnish Canadians--History--20th century. 3. Women immigrants--Canada--History--20th century. 4. Women--Canada--History--20th century. I. Title.

FC106.F5L572 2010   971.004'94541   C2010-904646-3

CONTENTS

Varpu Lindström

Author's Foreword

History of immigrant experience in Canada is a relatively new field. It developed in the seventies and eighties when Canadian history was rapidly expanding into new areas of study. The first challenger to the traditional political history and military history was labour history. This was soon followed by other forms of social history such as history of education, immigration and ethnic studies and finally history of women. The articles in this book were written while this exciting change in history was in its infancy. Suddenly kings, queens, prime ministers, and generals were competing for attention with domestic servants, lumber camp cooks, farm women, and labour activists. At the same time, multiculturalism became the new face of Canadian identity and feminist activity the rallying point of women seeking equality. In many ways the collected articles in this book reflect this shift in focus in Canadian history and society.

In 1986, the Multicultural History Society of Ontario published a pioneering, award-winning collection of articles on immigrant women entitled *Looking into My Sister's Eyes: An Exploration in Women's History.* Edited by Jean Burnet that book included my article "'I Won't Be a Slave!'" which was largely based on the research for my doctoral dissertation *Defiant Sisters: A Social History of the Finnish Immigrant Women in Canada 1890–1930,* which I defended also in 1986.

The current collection of articles is organized chronologically by subject matter. "Utopia for Women? The Sointula Experiment, 1901–1905" was originally a speech written for the centennial celebration of the historic utopian community of Sointula in British Columbia. The article was subsequently published in the *Journal of Finnish Studies*.

The article "The Radicalization of Finnish Farm Women in Northwestern Ontario, 1910–1930" was inspired by a remarkable woman, Taimi Davis, who also served as an inspiration in the award winning NFB documentary *Letters from Karelia: Father, Brother, Comrade, Spy,* directed by Kelly Saxberg. The article, published in 2001 in a CD-ROM entitled *Canada: Confederation to Present, an interactive history of Canada* by Chinook Multimedia and edited by Bob Hesketh and Chris Hackett, has not been previously available in printed format.

In 1996 Laurentian University hosted a conference on northern Ontario women. "Finnish Women's Experience in Northern Ontario Lumber Camps, 1920–1930" was published in the conference proceedings entitled *Changing Lives: Women in Northern Ontario* edited by Margaret Kechnie and Marge Reitsma-Street .

The last article in this book *Propaganda and Identity Construction:* "Media Representation in Canada of Finnish-Canadian Women during the Winter War of 1939–1940" was published in *Sisters or Strangers? Immigrant, Ethnic, and Racialized Women in Canadian* History edited by Marlene Epp, Franca Iacovetta, and Frances Swyripa and published by the University of Toronto Press in 2004. The research for the article is based on my book *From Heroes to Enemies: Finns in Canada, 1937–1947* published in 2000 by Aspasia Books.

Researching immigration and women's history has been a rewarding journey. For more than thirty years I have had the privilege of interviewing hundreds of women, shift through photo albums, and engross myself in the rich archival sources. I have been able to witness how immigration and ethnic history and women's studies grew into legitimized and respected disciplines. It has been a privilege to be part of this journey.

Varpu Lindström

Utopia for Women? The Sointula Experiment, 1901–1905

Nature has endowed Malcolm Island with stunning beauty. Vast vistas of the Pacific Ocean, snow capped mountains, and ancient forests are part of the scenery surrounding the small island situated off the coast of British Columbia towards the northern tip of Vancouver Island. In 1901, a group of forward-looking immigrants from Finland obtained the island from the Province of British Columbia. The Kalevan Kansa Colonization Company's plan was to create a harmonious utopian community based on co-operation and a mixture of theosophist and socialist beliefs. Much has been written about Sointula (Place of Harmony) and its turbulent first few years. Scholars have been attracted to the political philosophies of the island's two intellectual leaders, a romantic socialist theosophist Matti Kurikka (1863–1915) and his friend, a more pragmatic, Marxist-socialist, A.B. Mäkelä (1863–1932). Historians have described the establishment of the Kalevan Kansa Colonization Company, its newspaper *Aika*, the building of the colony's many dwellings, and the unfortunate commercial disasters that ultimately led to the collapse of the utopian experiment in 1905.[1] Many have also suggested that Matti Kurikka's views on women and marriage contributed to discord on the island. Critics of the experiment found accusations of "free love" a way to discredit the utopian experiment and to cast a shadow on the "immoral" women of Sointula.

As the community of Sointula prepared to celebrate its centennial, it was time to revisit its history. The focus of this article will be on Sointula's women. What kind of women dared to go to live in the most primitive conditions in Sointula? What was a socialist utopia supposed to offer for women? What were the expectations placed on women in building the community? What did equality of men and women mean a hundred years ago? What were Kurikka's actual views on marriage, childcare, and women's sexuality? Finally, how were women to achieve equality, independence, and freedom from society's patriarchal and repressive social norms?

Reinterpreting the Sointula legacy presents many challenges. It is easy to ascertain Kurikka's views of women as he published them in great detail in *Aika*. It is more difficult to know if women followed his advice and accepted his philosophy of life. The Sointula women's history must be pieced together from incomplete and fragmentary information.

BACKGROUND

At the end of the nineteenth century, Finland was an agricultural country with strong rural values. In 1900, 87 percent of the population lived on the land. As late as 1910, three quarters of all employed women were working in agriculture and only ten percent in industry and craft. Life in the northernmost corner of Europe was a constant struggle and frequent famines devastated the population. The "starvation years" of 1902–03 witnessed wide crop failures. Such harsh ecological conditions and self-sufficient economy has no place for the idle, weak woman. Every member of the society had to be productive if he/she hoped to survive over the long winter. Finnish women took part in all aspects of agriculture: they worked the fields, fished, hunted, gathered berries and mushrooms, took care of the domestic animals, and children. In such an environment communal values were strengthened as families, neighbours, and communities depended on each other for survival. A good woman was productive, skilled at all manner of domestic and agricultural production, frugal, and noncomplaining. Finns developed a stoic attitude to life and were reticent in displaying their emotions. They were close to nature and remnants of their former pantheistic nature religion could still be found in the daily beliefs, customs, and rituals of the rural people.[2]

The values of hard work, frugality, and sacrifice were supported by the strong Lutheran State Church to which well over ninety percent of the Finnish immigrants belonged. The church was also largely responsible for the literacy of its members as no parishioner was allowed to be confirmed if he/she did not know how to read the catechism. Without a certificate of confirmation one could not obtain an exit visa for emigration purposes. The compulsory public school system which educated boys and girls equally made sure that the younger immigrants were not only literate but had obtained several years of public school education.

The turn of the 20th century was full of political turbulence, and insecurity. Finland, which was a Grand Duchy of Russia, had enjoyed relative independence and its culture and language had flourished during the latter half of the nineteenth century. Artists and Finnish nationalists found inspiration in their ancient myths, which had been compiled in the national epic the *Kalevala*. The optimistic mood of the Finns changed with the repressive measures of russification practiced by the Czar, Nicholas II. One of his most hated commands was compulsory service for Finnish men in the Russian army. Many young sons chose the freedom and promise of "America" over the Russian army. Socialist and social democratic ideals were sweeping the country. Workers' organizations and halls were built as the literate and disgruntled population looked for new alternatives. The newspapers spread revolutionary ideas which questioned religious dogma, searched for socialist models that included, at least in theory, the emancipation of women. Some Finns concluded that the best economic, social, and political opportunities for new beginnings were outside of Finland, especially in North America.

The majority of Finnish emigrants sailing to North America were men who settled in the United States. Finnish emigration figures show that, between 1900 and 1904, over 74,000 emigrants left Finland of whom 36.3 percent were women.[3] In 1900, United States had over 62,000 people who were born in Finland.[4] In contrast, the 1901 census of Canada lists only 2,502 people of Finnish origin. The first reliable figures for British Columbia's Finnish population come from the 1911 census which indicates that only 32 percent of the Finns (900) were women.[5] Many of the women were wives, sisters, or daughters of Finnish men who had sponsored them over but a high percentage were also single women who came to work as domestic servants. In fact, of all Finnish emigrants before 1905 only about a quarter were family emigrants.[6] The rigors of emigration and the dreams of new beginnings were, by and large, for the healthy, single, and young men and women.

During the late nineteenth century Finnish immigrants began to settle in British Columbia where they worked as miners, loggers, and domestic servants. Other work opportunities for Finnish women revolved around servicing men in rooming houses, lumber camp kitchens, restaurants, or as bootleggers and prostitutes. Men's working conditions in Robert Dunsmuir's coal mines of North Wellington, Extension, and Ladysmith were dangerous and their life in the company towns insecure. To fight against isolation and alcoholism, and to improve the quality of their lives, the British Columbia immigrants organized temperance societies (1890), hand-written newspapers (1896), cultural activities, and a Lutheran congregation (1893). Some miners concluded, however, that these organizations could offer only small improvements and declared themselves ready for a more radical change—a utopian settlement.[7] Other Scandinavian groups had been successful in obtaining land from the province of British Columbia for experimental settlements. The Norwegians had chosen Bella Coola valley for their religious settlement in 1894. The Danes settled in Cape Scott in 1896, where they hoped to have a Danish settlement with local autonomy and freedom.[8] The Finnish miners decided to invite Matti Kurikka, a well-known believer in the possibilities of utopian settlement, to lead their utopian community.

Matti Kurikka, was a controversial intellectual in the literary circles of Finland, who was swept by the social, ideological, and political movements raging at the time. As a journalist, publicist, and editor of *Työmies* (Worker), he was in the centre of the socialist debate along with his associate editor, A.B. Mäkelä. Kurikka was an original thinker but he was also influenced by many philosophers and scientists. He was a theosophist who believed in the innate goodness of human beings and started to dream of a utopian settlement for Finnish people. He studied the co-operative settlement of "New Harmony" led by Robert Owen, was intrigued by the Oneida community of J.H. Noyes, admired the life philosophies and anti-clericalism of Leo Tolstoy and R.G. Ingersoll, the utopian ideas of French philosophers Fourier and Saint-Simon, lectured and translated from the works of Voltaire and Humboldt, and participated with keen interest in the literary salon of Finland's feminist author Minna Canth.[9] Ultimately he drafted his own plan for a *Kalevan Kansa* emigration society which he published in *Työmies*. Already in the society's first meeting, Kurikka's enthusiastic supporters decided to send him to Queensland, Australia in search of a place for a utopian settlement. Unfortunately, the *Chillagoe* settlement turned out to be a short-lived and ill-fated adventure from the beginning.[10]

Kurikka was glad to accept the invitation, complete with a promise of prepaid ticket from Australia to Canada. He arrived in Nanaimo full of optimism in August 1900. He became president of the *Kalevan Kansa* (People of Kaleva) Colonization Company and the plans for the establishment of a utopian settlement began immediately. His friend and colleague, A.B. Mäkelä, was summoned from Finland to help in the new adventure. In 1901, Kurikka started editing Canada's first Finnish-language newspaper, *Aika*, and on its pages painted a romantic and optimistic view of the new utopian community to be located on Malcolm Island. The British Columbia Finns found it hard to believe that the province actually gave them the island, which was 15 miles long and about 2½ miles wide (about 28,000 acres or 11,000 hectares), free of charge. It had a good supply of tall trees and they believed the

island offered possibilities for agriculture. It seemed ideal for the utopian settlement.[11]

Matti Kurikka (1863–1915) was the inspiration behind the utopian socialist
colony in Sointula, British Columbia (Archives of Ontario)

The Colonization Company recruited settlers directly from Finland and from North American Finnish communities where Kurikka toured, lectured, sang songs of Sointula, and sold *Aika* and other books to raise funds and recruit settlers. He was received with mixed emotions. Some dismissed him as a dreamer and a lunatic, others came to hear him out of curiosity, some warned that he was the devil incarnate, some were inspired by his romantic vision and charisma, and a few decided to take the bold step and follow him to Malcolm Island. Among those who dared to dream of a better world were also some women. A few women served as Kurikka's official recruiting agents and distributed *Aika*. On the list of his agents are some of the most prominent turn-of-the-century Finnish feminists in North America: Miss Elina Penttilä (Salem, Massachusetts), Miss Emmy Siltanen (St. Louis, Montana), Hanna Lehtinen (Brooklyn, New York), Anna Paulson (Rochester, New York), and Maggie J. Waltz (Calumet, Michigan). At least three of these women were single.[12]

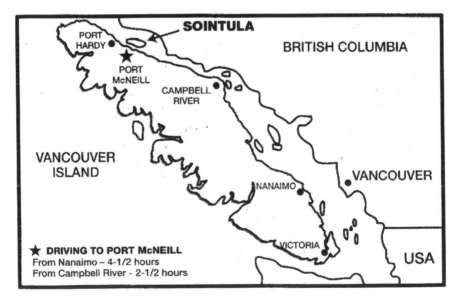

Perhaps the most active female agent for Sointula was Hanna Lehtinen who is described as a "travelling agent" and whose views of mother hood were published in *Aika*.[13] The most notable female agent was

Maggie Waltz (Margareeta 'Kreeta' Johanna Niranen), a journalist, businesswoman, temperance activist, feminist, and a suffragette, who later realized her dream of developing her own Finnish American colony. Her island utopia "Kreeta" (1905–1914) was located on Drummond Island in Lake Huron. A religious woman, Waltz disagreed with Kurikka's theosophist ideals and socialist beliefs and by 1904 she is no longer listed as his agent. Instead, Waltz's utopia was founded on temperance, religious principles, and capitalist cooperation.[14] Other women had more informal arrangements, but were nevertheless strong proponents of utopian ideas. For example three single women, Miina Ilkka, Manda Hankanen, and Ilma Jokilainen, who kept a rooming house in Ishpeming, Michigan, had been attracted to Kurikka's utopian ideals already in Finland. The women, collectively called the "Vaasa girls" because they were all from the province of Vaasa, spread Kurikka's teachings at the rooming house: V.J. Laaksonen, one of the early Sointula residents recalled: "After I met them (the Vaasa girls) I had my first lessons on Kalevan Kansa Colonization Company." Laaksonen was convinced that at least Manda Hankanen was in love with Kurikka, as well as his ideas.[15] Thus, some women were actively, and independently, sharing in the utopian dream.

Life in Sointula promised to be better for women. There were two basic tenets which guided the adopted views on women in Sointula. The first was that women were "equal in all respects" and the second was "natural law." The first woman to move to Sointula was Anna Wilander, who arrived during the early winter of 1902. She came from New York where she had just been married. Matti Halminen recalled: "Comrade [Anna] Wilander was asked to stay away from our boat and to come later with a larger boat, but this sprightly young woman was not afraid of danger and refused to stay behind. The boat trip the six newcomers made was most hazardous. We must wonder how they made it alive to their destination."[16] By March 1902 the island had fourteen men and Anna was their cook. The men were busy clearing fields and constructing buildings for the impending influx of settlers.

On June 3, 1902 Mrs. Salmi and Kaisa Riksman arrived with their four children. Kaisa Riksman recalled her first impressions:

> We arrived late at night. It was pitch black of course and all the bay was covered with these big kelps... The boat tied up to some sort of a slip and we had to walk along these logs to the shore where the shack was. In this log cabin there were five double bunks for all these families. Hay was piled on these bunks for a mattress, and my husband and I and the two children got one of these bunks for our own.[17]

Around the same time Mrs. Neva and Mrs. Lukkarinen and—very importantly for the women and children in the colony—Dr. Oswald H. Beckman also arrived. Dr. Beckman had owned a small hospital in Astoria, Oregon, and brought his medical equipment to Sointula. During the summer and fall of 1902, more settlers arrived drawn by the dream of a harmonious settlement where everything would be shared equally. An entire boatload of new settlers docked in time to celebrate midnight sun "Juhannus" on the island's new and hastily built "Cedar Hall."

During these festivities the settlement was officially named Sointula (Place of Harmony). In December 1902, the number of settlers in Sointula was 193 and a year later 238: a hundred men, fifty women, and 88 children. Most of the women were married. One of Sointula's problems was that there were only seven single women but 53 single men, including Matti Kurikka, who was divorced. As most boats brought in more single men and families, the arrival of the "Vaasa girls" and their entourage on June 16, 1903 was a welcome event.[18] This structural population imbalance, the shortage of single women, later became a source of social tension.[19]

The reality of Sointula life for women was harsh and full of adversity. The women's desire to remain on the island was severely tested. Communal living conditions were crude but offset by hope and great plans for improvement. A more difficult problem was the shortage of food, especially fresh milk for the children. The pastures of Sointula were too small and barren to feed the cows which had to be shipped to the mainland to graze. Some women found the hardships and communal living a difficult adjustment to make and left the island: "The winter of 1902 was a time of misery and of great trials. The wretched housing conditions made people, especially the women, dissatisfied, and members began slowly to move out of the island."[20] Disaster struck the community on 29 January 1903 when the main dwelling, a two-story log structure, caught fire killing eleven people and seriously injuring seventeen other residents who tried to jump out of the windows or rushed into the fire in desperate attempts to save their children. The community was devastated as it buried Maria Hantula and her four children, widow Maria Löfbacka and her two children, two Öberg children, and Victor Sortell. The following description of the fire and plight of the women and children was later published in *Canadan Uutiset*:

> From the ruins of the fire they found Mrs. Löfbacka. She had reached as far as the window at the top of the stairs with a child under each arm. And Mrs. Hantula with her youngest in her arms had reached the stairwell, presumably trying to get down but suffocating instead. Two other Hantula children were found under an iron bed and one on the bed. The sleeping children had fled the fire under the bed.[21]

Settlers had lost everything, their clothes, their books, their bedding. Many were left shivering in the wet and cold winter with only their night clothes on. The injured and burnt lived in tents together with the families who lost their living quarters. Eventually a shipment of clothing and blankets arrived from Vancouver along with two nurses. Despite all this calamity, holding on to their dreams of a better world, fifty women and their eighty-eight children remained in Sointula and a few more women arrived with each boatload of settlers. What then did Sointula promise its women?

EQUAL RIGHTS

Matti Kurikka and the Kalevan Kansa Colonization Company promised that in Sointula "men and women are equal in all respects."[22] Kaisa Riksman emphasized the uniqueness of the equality: "I think the main idea was to have a free society. They especially emphasized that women should have equal rights with men. At that time women had no property rights, and they had no rights whatsoever in wages."[23] The by-laws of the Kalevan Kansa Colonization Company divided its members into two categories: internal and external. All members who worked for the colony at least 150 days a year and lived on the island were considered internal members regardless of sex and given member's privileges, including use of land.

At a time when suffrage battles were still ongoing, the women in Sointula gained an equal right to vote (1902) and a right to participate fully in the governance of the community. They were not only allowed, but expected to speak up at meetings and to have an equal role in making decisions concerning communal life. The Board of Directors, however, continued to be men. It was understood that women had some catching up to do in their political training and that they needed to organize. Soon sewing circles evolved into "study rings" where Sointula women practiced minute-taking, public speaking, and debating. It is not clear exactly when the Sointula women's organization was founded but it was active in 1904. The Sointula women were not only interested in improving their own condition but wished to take an active role in organizing a national network of women. They planned to be leaders rather than followers. Far from feeling isolated or marginalized, the women of Sointula celebrated International Women's Day on March 8, sent petitions to Ottawa, collected funds for women's causes, and sought international links.

In their meetings women also passed resolutions that they brought to the Kalevan Kansa Colonization Company meetings. Women had been attracted to Sointula because it promised to be a colony that was free from alcohol. This to them meant also freedom from physical abuse in the hands of drunken husbands. But the women's committee resolved to ban swearing and smoking as well. The last two resolutions were, however, too much for some men in Sointula. An article in *Aika*, signed by "Sointula women," on this topic received an angry and cynical rebuke from A.B. Mäkelä (Austin McKela) who reminded the women that there was no proof that smoking was harmful and that swearing was not nearly as damaging as rumour-mongering.[24]

All women in Sointula were expected to work eight hours a day and everyone in the colony received the same wage—one dollar a day—regardless of the nature of the work. The work was still mainly divided by gender with women working in the communal kitchen and the laundry, in farming, sewing, healthcare, and midwifery. The women's work was determined by a special committee composed of women, which divided the tasks.[25]

In the annual report of 1903 it was recognized, however, that until such time as the community was able to organize childcare, "a troubling difference in women's work responsibilities remained" and women with several children would have to be exempted from their communal work duties.[26] If women wished they could also participate in other aspects of work such as fishing, logging, and construction, but few did. With equal pay came also equal financial responsibilities. When the colony was in financial trouble women were expected to contribute. The chair of the fundraising committee was Henni Österberg and the secretary Ida Illberg. They planned a great lottery in aid of the community and especially towards its childcare centre. They offered to raffle their jewelry, which was considered not to have any place in Sointula. Unfortunately the province refused to give them a lottery license.[27]

SOCIAL SECURITY

Internal membership guaranteed a right to work, a plot of land, and security in sickness and old age. This was particularly important to immigrant women who had seen too many examples of the miserable conditions that single mothers with children had to endure after family break-up, illness, accident, or death took their spouse away. Paragraph #22 of the by-laws promised a worry-free future:

> All internal members and their dependents will be fed and housed in the event of illness and disability. If an internal member dies, all the member's privileges will be transferred to the spouse to use for the spouse's benefit and for the benefit of the family of the deceased.[28]

One of the promises of Sointula was that the vulnerable of all ages would be taken care of and all would live together in peaceful harmony. This message was spread effectively through music during Kurikka's recruitment tours. One of the theme songs of Sointula, written by Kurikka himself, was entitled "Kaleva's People" and sung to the well-known melody of "Santa Lucia."[29]

> *Kaleva's People*
> Aallotar once again, clear its reflection
> See how the gust of wind swishes the branches.
> Gone now is finally roar of the storming,
> Gone is the agony of waves a-crashing.
> Oh how harmonious, Oh it is wonderful!
> Now rejoice my dear ones, Kaleva's People!
> There are our fertile fields, ploughed by our people
> There are the cattle bells, beautifully ringing.
> There are our ships afloat, cleaving the ocean,
> There all its children now, play, jump and holler.
> Oh how harmonious, etc.
> Look at the elderly, who sit there resting,
> Look at the invalid, tied to a wheelchair.
> Hear now my sister sing, humming and cooing,
> Look how the menfolk too dress up for wooing.
> Oh how harmonious, etc.
> That is our people's base, its sound foundation,
> Those are the mighty words, nature's directions:
> Forest and breezy wind, children a-playing,
> Green fields and cattle bells, greybeards a-resting.
> Oh how harmonious, etc.
> *Translated by Börje Vähämäki*

FREEDOM FROM CHILDCARE

Kurikka argued that equal rights could be achieved only if women were guaranteed certain freedoms: freedom from childcare, freedom to control their own bodies, freedom from church and other patriarchal conventions, freedom from marriage, and freedom to love according to the laws of nature. In Kurikka's view women deserved not only freedom from childcare but children also deserved the best possible education. It was the community's duty to sacrifice for and invest in its children. All adults in the community were responsible for providing the community's children of all ages the best possible, progressive upbringing, healthcare, and nourishment for both body and soul. Sports, art, and music were thought to be vital ingredients for the development of a balanced soul. To achieve this, a daycare centre was needed. The devastating fire, and several other building projects delayed the opening of the long-planned daycare centre until the end of March 1904. When the centre opened thirty children enrolled immediately. The centre was depicted as "the most beautiful building on the island" with three spacious and light rooms and a dry playground. The "professionals" who cared for the children were Lempi and Martti Myrtti. They are described as kind-hearted, conscientious, and experienced educators. In 1904, Kurikka declared that "all the most progressive mothers have offered their children to be brought up by the community."[30] Children could be left for daycare in the morning and picked up at night or they could board at the centre. All food and clothing was provided by the community free of charge if the children were boarders. In 1904, there were approximately seventy young children in Sointula. An unidentified group-portrait from 1904 (see p. 23) found in the Sointula Museum depicts over sixty healthy-looking, immaculately dressed, boys and girls ranging in age from small infants to young teenagers.[31]

These "new progressive ideas" of childcare were not easy for mothers who did not wish to have "freedom" from childcare. Articles in *Aika* in 1904 published by "Sointula Women" speak of the difficulty mothers had in giving up their children to the school. It was described as the ultimate sacrifice but also the only choice a truly liberated and progressive mother had. Scornful articles by Kurikka argued that it was selfish for mothers to keep their children at home and deny them the best possible learning experience. Mothers were not the best educators for their children. Children required patience, they needed consistency, and they needed to be heard. Mothers were often too busy to

give their children full attention and too tired to be patient. It was easier to give in to the children's demands than to be consistent. The
childcare centre provided "education from beginning to end," preparing children for life's challenges. If women truly loved their children,
Kurikka argued, they would give them up to professional childcare
workers.[32]

For thirty-seven older children, a new, red, two-room schoolhouse
was opened in the fall of 1904. Kalevan Kansa Colonization Company,
as part of its agreement with the province of British Columbia was
obliged to build and maintain an English-language public school. Miss
Cleveland had the first challenge of teaching the Sointula children,
who until then had only been taught in Finnish.[33] Overall, Sointula was
a child-friendly community. It was understood that ultimately only the
children will truly understand the utopian principles of harmonious co-
existence and only they can build a true utopia. The parents who were
products of capitalist "priest-ridden" society, found it impossible to
shake off all the vestiges of their repression. In the daycare centre and
in the community, children were taught to be free from conventions
and to obey natural law.

FREEDOM TO CONTROL THEIR OWN BODIES

Kurikka believed that women alone had the right to control their
bodies. A woman's body belonged to her, not her husband, and her
soul belonged to the Deity, not to any organized church. Women (and
men) needed freedom from the church and freedom from convention.
Kurikka's explanations of women's body, sexuality, health require-
ments, and male-female sexual relations drew heavily on Dr. Foote's
Medical Encyclopaedia. Kurikka also cited Dr. Alice B. Stockmann's
book, *Tokology*, and Dr. Rosch.[34] Ultimately, however, Kurikka's
advice to women, as published in *Aika*, is his own theosophist interpretation of the "natural law" that controls humans. Kurikka declared
that the people of Sointula would be free citizens in free bodies.
According to Kurikka, "a woman who has intercourse on her
husband's terms, for his benefit, to please him, is a victim of prosti-

tution." Hence marriage is an unnatural arrangement. The church, which forces women to subjugate themselves and their bodies to one man, is an accomplice in the enslavement of women. "A woman who does not allow nature to take its course because of religious taboos, society's taboos, or fear of pregnancy, is a victim of double morality." Institutionalized religion forces women (and men) to swear false oaths of life-long fidelity which, according to Kurikka, are impossible to keep. Monogamy is unnatural, and fidelity leads to a master-slave relationship.

Since marriage is "an erroneous interpretation of Jesus' will" Kurikka encouraged the people of Sointula to "undo the unnatural marriages among us ... let us respect the freedom to love—let us break the shackles of marriage." Divorce would free women to seek new partners. If, however, a woman wished to have a permanent living arrangement with a man, Kurikka strongly recommended that she should not live with her lover; she should live with a friend.[35]

FREEDOM FROM CONVENTION: NATURAL LAW

In a series of articles published in *Aika* in 1903–1904, Kurikka explained in detail his interpretation of the law of nature. At the same time he used the pages of his newspaper to provide sex education to the colony. He wanted the people of Sointula to be able to speak normally, without slander or derision, about intercourse. He frequently quoted "experts" and used scientific terminology to make his points.[36]

Kurikka's main message was that nature contradicts convention but that nature does not make mistakes. It was necessary, therefore, to expose the taboos imposed by convention, to break the barriers to natural behaviour, and to create new structures in support of natural law. At a time when other Canadian women were taught Victorian ideals of womanhood—modesty, purity, morality—and told that it was their duty to satisfy men's desires, the women of Sointula were told that according to natural law men and women had equal desires. Intercourse should never be imposed but had to be based on "voluntary giving." Kurikka urged: "Let women decide what to do with their bodies according to laws of nature."

Portrait of Sointula children 1904 (Sointula Museum collection)

The physical attraction between men and women, according to Kurikka, was based on "electricity." The theory of electricity implied that opposites attract. Hence men and women should not live too close together as they would become too familiar with each other, and this familiarity would make them too similar and less able to "produce electricity."

The exchange of energy between a man and a woman had to be a "natural contract," based on free will of both man and woman. In fact, such an exchange was necessary, even obligatory, in order to strengthen both body and soul and live a healthy life. If a husband and wife continued to have intercourse after they no longer felt electricity it would lead to illness, infections, degeneration in the offspring, and eventually death. Convention, however, contradicted nature and had made natural behaviour impossible. Men and women were ready for "production of electricity" at fifteen but society insisted that they suppress it. Suppression of electricity, according to this theory, lead to denial, illness, aggression, and ultimately to double morality, including prostitution. Conventions created guilt, shame, secrets, and lies. These conventions imposed by church and patriarchy would be abolished from Sointula and along with them prostitution, venereal disease, and double morality.[37]

ACCOMMODATING THE LAW OF NATURE IN SOINTULA

It was not enough for Kurikka to expose the taboos and explain his theories of natural behaviour between men and women. He wanted to create structures to accommodate the new utopian society based on harmonious co-existence and freedom from taboos. He realized that women needed the support of the community. His far-reaching plans included free healthcare and hospitals for everyone and healthcare and private facilities for pregnant and nursing women. Kurikka believed that co-operative care would help women to have happy, healthy, clean, and constructive birthing experiences. If women, however, wished to stay home while pregnant, Kurikka of course allowed them the freedom to do so, but strongly implored them to come to the health centre to give birth and to stay there for at least one month, but preferably until they finished breast feeding. After this, if they truly loved their children, mothers would give them to the childcare professionals.

Privacy for all women should be safeguarded. Kurikka was adamant in declaring that people's private lives were not the community's business but everyone's private business. Women should not be asked how they became pregnant. There should be absolutely no discrimination between married, divorced, or single women. The Kalevan Kansa Colonization Company should not deal with couples at all, b,ut with individuals. Women are the best judges of their bodies, their health needs, and their desires and should be the only ones making those decisions. This way, women could achieve natural (sexual) freedom and control of their bodies.

Kurikka believed that women were unable to produce electricity after birth and while breast feeding. In most cases, "only after the child is given away does the production of electricity begin anew." If, however, the electricity began to pulsate while women were breast feeding, they should stop the breast feeding and go and take care of their "electrical impulses" by seeking new relationships and leaving their children to communal care.[38]

THE UTOPIAN EXPERIMENT ENDS

The ideals on which the Kalevan Kansa Colonization Company was built—harmonious co-existence, altruism, equally shared response-bility, communal living, freedom from convention, natural law, and equality of men and women—were severely tested by the harsh reality of life on Malcolm Island. Too many people came too fast causing the colony to have a constant shortage of housing and thus primitive living conditions. The island was not as suitable for agriculture as the colonists had hoped and people had to seek employment off the island. The Kalevan Kansa Colonization Company entered into construction contracts that turned unprofitable, even disastrous. Men were tired after months of hard labour for no monetary benefit. When they returned home to Malcolm Island they were dismayed to learn of Kurikka's series of articles on marriage and "electricity." They were particularly distressed that some wives had decided to end relationships which no longer had "electricity".

Rumours of "free love" were rampant and were spread with glee by the enemies of the utopian experiment. It did not help that Kurikka sent his thoughts on natural law to both Finnish and English language newspapers sparking further interest and debate. Kurikka was a handsome man with intense piercing eyes and abundant charisma. It was easy to imagine women falling for his eloquent speeches and romantic notions. One persistent rumour that followed Kurikka wherever he lectured was that "every woman who wanted to join Kalevan Kansa had to sleep with Kurikka for three nights before she was granted full membership."[39] In the middle of one of Kurikka's recruitment speeches in Ishpeming, Michigan, for example, an elderly matron got up and, as she was leaving the premises, exclaimed: "I would not sleep a single night beside such a dark devil."[40] Kurikka himself was well aware of his charisma and his attractiveness to the opposite sex. In November 1904, he wrote to his daughter:

> In this country [Canada] where relations between the sexes are free beyond all restraint, I have observed that if I wanted to misuse my electric influences, which I possess in great measure, against young, inexperienced women, the most delicate would helplessly become my victims.[41]

One of the women who briefly embraced the natural law concept was A.B. Mäkelä's wife Elli. This caused an irreparable rift between the idealistic Kurikka and his pragmatic, now vengeful colleague. Kurikka concedes that ultimately his progressive ideas about women's sexual equality were partially responsible for the deep divisions in the community:

> The main reason for this split ... is female emancipation. As a result of my writing many wives started to oppose the passionate advances of their husbands and the latter became angry and jealous and in the end believed that their wives had fallen in love with me and for that reason

betrayed them. Everything that was already bad on the island became exacerbated because of this.[42]

A few other single and married women are identified as practicing Kurikka's teachings of "free love". Several men, especially the younger members of the colony, also professed to be ardent supporters of these revolutionary ideas. Most women and couples, however, continued along the old conventions and the "free love" of Sointula seems to have existed, more or less, mostly on the ideological level. Some felt the unnatural gender imbalance in Sointula lead Kurikka to dream of "sharing the women." Others thought he was abusing his powers and self-serving. The issue was hotly debated in a special meeting that ultimately divided the community into two factions, Kurikka's supporters and those who condemned his free-love teachings and supported Mäkelä.[43]

No doubt the particular reality of Sointula provided an important context to Kurikka's ideals of women. These ideals developed and changed considerably during the Sointula experiment as Kurikka was able to identify with many women's needs. At the same time, he too was a victim of conventions, and when he was feeling down he had difficulty in believing in the potential of women. He sometimes blamed his troubles on undisciplined, quarreling, rumour-mongering women who still needed to be civilized and educated. Ultimately, Kurikka and his supporters lost the trust of the Sointula residents and Kurikka was no longer welcome to stay on the island. When he left Sointula, many of his most ardent followers also moved elsewhere. The remaining community of forty-five men, twenty women and forty children tried as best they could to carry on. On 27 May 1905, the Kalevan Kansa Colonization Company was liquidated.[44]

CONCLUSION

While the "natural law" debate of Sointula has raised much interest, Kurikka's dream for the equality of women was significantly broader. In Sointula, women had equal legal and political rights, including equal pay for a day's work. They were promised a safe and clean environment free from alcohol, violence, and brutality. In many ways Kurikka's visionary views were more than a hundred years ahead of his times. Women are still battling for equal pay for equal work; they are demanding longer maternity leaves, guaranteed daycare, and the right to control their own bodies. Although better educated than men, women are under-represented in politics, they work in female ghettoes, and they earn much less than men. Alcoholism, smoking, and drugs continue to be a major social problem, as does family violence and prostitution. "No" means "no" is a slogan that still needs defending.

For one hundred years, since the founding of Sointula, emancipated women have endured considerable ridicule. First the objects of derision were the suffragettes, later the women's liberationists, and currently the radical feminists. Each step on the ladder of equal rights has proven to be a hard-fought battle and many battles remain for the new millennium. If Kurikka's ideas are too radical for today's society, then the Sointula experiment and its agenda for women was truly exceptional and revolutionary considered in its historical context. That some strong Finnish immigrant women dared to believe a hundred years ago in "the equality of men and women in every respect" is inspirational. That they were willing to act on their beliefs and to build a community based on their dreams is unique in the annals of Canadian history.

The fact that the experiment failed, does not diminish the vision and courage of the pioneering women of Sointula. Instead of respect and understanding, they endured unspeakable hardships, earned the ridicule and scorn of many of their contemporaries, and were silenced by the future generations. The centennial celebrations of Sointula afford the community and scholars an opportunity to resurrect the unique and interesting history of the women (and men) of Malcolm Island.

This article was first published in the Journal of Finnish Studies, Volume 4, Number 2, December 2000, pp. 4–25. *It is republished here with permission of the* Journal of Finnish Studies.

ENDNOTES

---

[1] Aili Anderson, *History of Sointula* (Sointula: Sointula Centennial Committee, 1969); Matti Halminen, *Sointula: Kalevan Kansan ja Kanadan Suomalaisten Historiaa* (Helsinki: 1936); John Ilmari Kolehmainen, "Harmony Island: A Finnish Utopian Venture in British Columbia," *British Columbia Historical Quarterly*, Vol. V., No. 2. 111–23; A. H. Salo, "Kalevan Kansa Colonization Company: Finnish Millenarian Activity in B.C." M.A. thesis, University of British Columbia, 1978; Paula Wild, *Sointula: Island Utopia* (Madeira Park: Harbour Publishing, 1995); J. Donald Wilson, "A synoptic view of the *Aika*, Canada's first Finnish Language Newspaper," *Amphora* , No. 39 (March, 1980) 9–14; "Matti Kurikka and A. B. Mäkelä: Socialist Thought among Finns in Canada, 1900–1932," *Canadian Ethnic Studies*, X , No.2 (1978) 9–21; and "'Never Believe What You Have Never Doubted': Matti Kurikka's Dream for a New World Utopia," in Michael G. Karni ed., *Finnish Diaspora I: Canada, South America, Africa, Australia, and Sweden* (Toronto: Multicultural History Society of Ontario, 1981) 31–53; and "Coal Miners and Socialists: Finns in British Columbia Before World War I," *Polyphony,* Vol. 3 No. 2 (Fall, 1981) 55 64.

[2] For information in English on the history of women in Finland see, Satu Apo, et al., *Women in Finland* (Helsinki: Otava Publishing Co. Ltd., 1999) and Merja Manninen and Päivi Setälä eds., *The Lady with a Bow: The Story of Finnish Women* (Helsinki: Otava Publishing Co. Ltd., 1990).

[3] Reino Kero, *Migration from Finland to North America in the Years between the United States Civil War and the First World War* (Turku: Institute of Migration, 1974) 91.

[4] Jouni Korkiasaari, *Suomalaiset maailmalla* (Turku: Institute of Migration, 1989) 28.

[5] Statistics Canada, Censuses of Canada, 1901 and 1911.

[6] Kero, *Migration from Finland to North America*, 121.

7. Halminen, *Sointula,* 10–15.

[8] Gordon Fish, *Dreams of Freedom: Bella Coola, Cape Scott, Sointula, Sound Heritage Series*, number 36 (Provincial Archives of British Columbia: Victoria, B.C., 1982) 1–30; see also Justine Brown, *All Possible Worlds: Utopian Experiments in British Columbia* (Vancouver: New Star Books, 1995).

[9] Kalevi Kalemaa, *Matti Kurikka legenda jo eläessään* (Helsinki:WSOY, 1978); Kurikka refers to their views in his articles in *Aika* and translates sections of Voltaire, Ingersoll and Humboldt in 1903–1904.

[10] Olavi Koivukangas, *Sea, Gold and Sugarcane: Finns in Australia 1851–1947* (Turku, Finland: Institute of Migration, 1986) 83–93; Teuvo Peltoniemi, *Kohti Parempaa Maailmaa: Suomalaisten ihannesiirtokunnat 1700-luvulta nykypäivään* (Helsinki: Otava, 1985) 31–40.

[11] Halminen, *Sointula*, 34.

[12] This list is compiled from agents listed on the back page of *Aika,* 1903–1904.

[13] Hanna Lehtinen from Brooklyn, New York, is listed as a travelling agent in *Aika,* 1 December 1903 and her article "Toivotan onnea" (My congratulations) on childcare is in *Aika*, 1 June 1904, 433–37.

[14] Carl Ross and K. Marianne Wargelin Brown, *Women Who Dared: The History of Finnish American Women* (St. Paul, Minnesota: Immigration History Research Center, 1986) 151–57.

[15] V. J. Laaksonen, "Muutamia oikaisuja ja huomautuksia Matti Halmisen Sointula teokseen" (Some corrections to and remarks of Matti Halminen's *Sointula* book). Typewritten manuscript dated in Ladysmith, B.C., 29 September 1951. Finnish Canadian Historical Society Collection, Ontario Archives.

[16] Halminen, *Sointula*, 62.

17
Kaisa Riksman's interview is quoted in Fish, *Dreams of Freedom*, 35; the original is in the Sointula Museum Archives.

18
V. J. Laaksonen, who arrived as part of the "Vaasa girls" group, brought along his wife and daughter. Typewritten manuscript.

19
Halminen, *Sointula*, 109; Varpu Lindström, *Defiant Sisters: A Social History of Finnish Immigrant Women in Canada 1890–1930* (Toronto: Multicultural History Society of Ontario, 1986) 22–31.

20
Halminen, *Sointula*, 64; Lindström, *Defiant Sisters*, 30–31; Anderson, *History of Sointula*, 7.

21
Canadan Uutiset, 13 October 1927.

22
Aika, 1 June 1904, 429.

23
See endnote 17.

24
Aika, "Tasan uhraukset" (Even sacrifices) by Sointulan naiset (Sointula's women) 15 May 1904, 404–06 and "Muistutus" (Reminder) by Austin McKela (A. B. Mäkelä), 406–07.

25
Halminen, *Sointula*, 76.

26
Halminen quotes the 1903 annual report of Kaleva Colonization Company in *Sointula*, 108.

27
Aika, 15 April 1904, 342–43 and 347; *Aika* 15 June 1904, 28.

28
Kalevan Kansan Säännöt (By-Laws of the Kalevan Kansa), 8 November 1901, 8.

29
The original in Finnish was published in a song book *Kalevan Kansan Sointuja I, V. 1903, Sointula, B.C.* (Vancouver, 1903), 13; and later in Matti Kurikka, *Elämän Sointuja* (Helsinki: Vihtori Kososen Kirjapaino, 1908), 23. Translation is by Börje Vähämäki, as presented at Sointula seminar, 2000.

30
A series of articles in *Aika* discuss the issue of childcare in Sointula: Matti Kurikka, "Lasten-koti" 1 April 1904, 289–95;"Elämän ohjeita Kalevan Kansalle" (Instructions for Life to the Kalevan Kansa People) 15 June 1904, 9–10 and "Lapset" (Children), 12–16; "Lapset" (continued) 1 July 1904, 44–48. See also an article by Hanna Lehtinen "Toivotan Onnea" (My Congratulations) 1June 1904, 433–37.

31
Sointula Museum Collection. A photography studio was established on the island in March 1904. It advertises group portraits of the children of Kalevan Kansa in the 15 March 1904 issue of *Aika, 285.*

32
See for example, *Aika*, 15 June 1904, 9–10.

33
J. Donald Wilson, "The Socialist Legacy on Malcolm Island after the Collapse of the Utopian Settlement of Sointula," *Melting into Great Waters: Papers from FinnForum V*, a special issue of *Journal of Finnish Studies*, Vol. 1, No. 3 (December 1997) 156–67.

34
Kurikka was fascinated by Dr. Alice B. Stockmann's book *Tokology* which he recommends to "every unmarried maiden." See for example *Aika* 15 March 1904, 277–283; Kurikka found Dr. Foote's medical advice helpful in his sex education articles. See *Aika*, 15 April 1904, 326–28.

35
See Kurikka's articles on "Avio-kysymys" (Marriage question), *Aika*, 15 March 1904, 277–283; 1 April 1904, 299–304; 15 April 1904, 326–28; 1 May 1904, 394–401; 1 June 1904, 422–24.

36
See footnote 35 and *Aika*, 15 April 1904, 326–28.

37
Kurikka discusses his views of "electricity" (which are borrowed from Dr. Foote) for example in *Aika*, 1 June 1904, 417–31.

38
These views are explained most clearly in *Aika*, 1 June 1904, "Ihanne-avioliitto"(Ideal marriage) 428–31.

[39] V. J. Laaksonen, "Muutamia oikaisuja ja huomautuksia Matti Halmisen Sointula teokseen" (Some corrections to and remarks on Matti Halminen's *Sointula* book). Typewritten manuscript dated in Ladysmith, B.C., 29 September 1951. Finnish Canadian Historical Society Collection, Ontario Archives.

[40] Ibid.

[41] Letter from Matti Kurikka to his daughter Aili, in Linnoila Collection, November 1904 as cited in J. Donald Wilson, "Matti Kurikka and the Settlement of Sointula, British Columbia, 1901–1905" 18.

[42] Ibid.

[43] V.J. Laaksonen manuscript.

[44] J. Donald Wilson, "The Socialist Legacy on Malcolm Island, 155"; Halminen, *Sointula*,

"I Won't Be a Slave!"
Finnish Domestics in Canada, 1911–30

It is with deep sorrow and longing that I inform you of the death of my
beloved daughter Siiri Mary who became the victim of a terrible death
in her place of employment in Nanaimo, B.C. on the first of May at
04:00 in the morning. As she was lighting the fire in the kitchen stove
with kerosene it exploded and the fire ignited her clothes and she burnt so badly
that on the fifth of May she died in the Nanaimo hospital at
11:30 in the evening. She was born on January 1, 1906 and died
on May 5, 1922 at the age of 16 years 4 months and 4 days.
Father remembers you with bitter sadness and longing.[1]

This touching funeral notice reveals some of the dark realities
about domestic service in Canada. Why was the sixteen-year-
old girl having to start her work day at 4:00 A.M.? What
knowledge did she have of kerosene? And what protection in case of
an accident? Who could she turn to for advice, or what avenues for
complaint did she have? While the domestic servant looked after all
the members and guests of the household, who looked after her? These
questions were hotly debated in the various organizations established
for Finnish maids in North America. Despite the many negative aspects of domestic work, it was the most common occupation for Finnish immigrant women.

The domestics themselves are quick to point out the many positive
features about their life as a *haussi-meiti* (housemaid). From the discussions emerge important differences in the society's view of domestic service as a low-status occupation and the maid's own view of her

work. This article will probe into both the positive and negative aspects of life as a domestic, taking the examination beyond the work place and into the community. In the process the study will discuss the organizations and communication networks which were established to assist the Finnish domestic servants.

SUPPLY AND DEMAND

A University of Toronto probe into the conditions of female labour in Ontario in 1889 noted that the demand for domestic servants exceeded the supply and that it was necessary to import domestic servants from the British Isles.[2] Barber's thorough examination of the recruitment and settlement of the British domestic servants as the most welcome women shows to what great extent the government and employers would go to recruit domestics.[3] Young girls, often orphans from England, were brought to Canada through various benevolent agencies and ended up as domestic servants.[4] Still, as poignantly illustrated by Makeda Silvera's book *Silenced,* the chronic shortage of domestic servants has continued until the present day.[5] There have, of course, been periodic fluctuations in the demand, and some communities felt the shortage of domestic workers more severely than others, but generally the supply of maids did not meet the demand.

After the turn of the century, Finnish domestics were enticed to come to Canada. The federal government bent immigration regulations, created special categories and made easier travel arrangements for women who promised to work as domestic servants.[6] In fact, it was the only category, in addition to farm worker, in which a single woman from Finland during the twenties was allowed to enter the country.[7] Like the British, they too were welcome. The following riddle in a Finnish paper illustrates the point:

> I am not beautiful,
> Yet, I am the most wanted woman.
> I am not rich,
> Yet I am worth my weight in gold.
> I might be dull, stupid,
> Dirty and mean,

> Yet, all the doors are open for me.
> I am a welcome guest
> All of the elite compete for me.
> I am a maid.[8]

Finnish women entered the industry during its "transitional period," when the proportional importance of domestic service as a major occupation for women was declining. In 1921, domestics represented only 18 percent of all employed women in Canada. New opportunities were enticing Canadian women away from domestic service and the resulting gap was partially filled by newly arrived immigrants.[9] The largest proportion of foreign domestic workers still came from the British Isles—75 percent before World War One and 60 percent during the 1920s.[10] Among the other ethnic groups, the Scandinavians and Finns showed an exceptionally high propensity for domestic work. While the British women, who were able to speak English, also had other opportunities for employment, the Finnish women were almost exclusively concentrated in the service industry. In Finnish jargon "going to work in America" became synonymous with "going to be a domestic servant in America."[11] During the twenties, the Finnish domestic servants made up 7–8 percent of all female immigrants classified as "female domestics." In the fiscal year ending 31 March 1929, for example, 1,288 Finnish women arrived in Canada under this category out of a total of 1,618 adult female immigrants from Finland.[12] This does not necessarily mean that all women actually settled into their declared occupations in Canada. In fact, the Finnish Immigrant Home Records indicate that there was considerable diversity of skills among these "excellent domestic servants." Letters of recommendation from Finland often included revealing additions such as "she is also an experienced seamstress," or "this woman is a skilful masseuse."[13] The domestic service category was simply the most convenient for immigration purposes.

Nevertheless, the vast majority of working women in Finnish communities were maids. Calculations based on the two largest urban centres indicate that of all the Finnish immigrant women employed outside the home during the twenties at least 66 percent were maids in

Toronto and Montreal.[14] Except for a handful of women who worked in restaurants, "all Finnish women in Winnipeg were maids."[15] This single, overpowering concentration of Finnish women in domestic work had a great impact on the community which had to adapt to the life patterns of the maids. Just as mining, lumbering and construction work coloured the life of the Finnish men, influenced their economic status, settlement location and political thinking, domestic work shaped the world-views of the Finnish women.

The nature of domestic service was also changing from the pre-dominance of live-in maids around the turn of the century to "day workers" by the depression. For example, the percentage of laun-dresses in the service occupations doubled between 1901 and 1911.[16] It was becoming increasingly difficult to find women willing to live in and, consequently, more of this work was left to the newly arrived immigrants—the greenhorns—whose occupational choices were lim-ited. The Finnish women knew upon arrival that there would be no problem in finding a job. "I could have worked thirty hours a day, eight days a week," commented one tired woman;[17] and a man shame-fully recollected:

> There was no work for me, nothing, but my wife was always able to get work as a live-in cook. What to do? I had to take women's work. Oh, I didn't like it. I was to look after the liquor, but in the morning I had to do some dusting too. I hated women's work and the pay was not good either, but we had a place to live and food to eat. As soon as I could get man's work, I left.[18]

The consequent role reversal, which heightened during periods of economic slow-down, was a bitter pill for many men to swallow. "My mother worked," remembered a dynamic leader of the Finnish com-munity, "she could always find work in the houses, and my father stayed home with the children." Then she laughed, "He never liked it, but he did a good job!"[19] By 1928 when the Great Depression had hit the lumbering industry—one of the biggest employers of Finnish men —the frustrated "house-husband" syndrome spread beyond the urban centres. Letters to Finland explained how "women are the only ones who find work and men stay home to look after the children."[20]

Women gained in status as "they were the only ones with money to spend."[21] Even during the depression in 1937 when all doors to immigration were shut, the government launched a special scheme to bring in "Scandinavian and Finnish Domestics." Most of the women who came under this plan were Finnish and in their late twenties and early thirties.[22]

Thus, the Finnish women who came to Canada from 1900-30 when the supply of domestics was dwindling and the demand for live-in maids still strong were in a good economic position. They came mainly as single, mature women who were used to hard work, and many had been domestics prior to emigrating. This combination, the availability of work and the ability to do it, was the main reason why Finnish women, both in the United States and Canada, were found in such large numbers in domestic service. In addition, there were other positive features about domestic work which attracted the newcomers.

THE BRIGHT SIDE OF DOMESTIC WORK

The most pressing concerns of newly arrived immigrants included where to live and where to work. As a live-in maid both worries were taken care of at once. While the Finnish men spent much of their first years in Canada in rooming-houses or bunk-houses, or roaming around in search of work, the live-in maids at least had a solid roof over their heads. Their homes might only be damp cellar quarters, or, more commonly, cold upstairs rooms, but they could also be sunny rooms in luxurious mansions, with beautiful gardens and comfortable feather beds. Lice-covered blankets, hair frozen to the bunk-house wall, or the unpalatable smell of dozens of sweaty socks were not part of the maid's experience. Instead, the domestics usually lived in middle- and upper-class homes in safe and relatively clean neighbourhoods. No time was spent looking for housing and no initial investment needed to buy furniture or basic kitchen utensils.

The maid's limited free time was carefully monitored by the employers. "The family" was sure to report any unexpected absences or late arrivals of the maids. In case of serious trouble or illness at least someone would notice and beware. The stories of unidentified Finnish men found dead by the railroad tracks, lost in the bush, or dying alone from an illness did not have their female counterparts. Someone, whether from reasons of moral concern or meanness, was keeping tabs on the maid's whereabouts and routines. For many younger women, the employers became the surrogate family, disciplining and restricting their social activities. This, of course, was a double-edged sword. One summer evening when a Finnish maid in Toronto failed to come home from the local dance at the agreed-upon time of eleven, the employers swiftly called the police. In her case the alarm was too late as her beaten-up body was found on the outskirts of Toronto in 1916, but her friend was saved from a similar fate.[23] While appreciating any genuine concern, many women resented the strict scheduling of their free time. A Port Arthur maid remembers her first evening off in 1910:

> I have been rebellious ever since I was a child. On my only evening off, I was supposed to be back at 10:00 P.M. Well, I went to the hall to see a play and to dance afterwards and didn't get back until one in the morning. I found the door bolted from inside and my blood rushed to my head. They treated me just as if I was a small child incapable of looking after my own affairs. I banged on that door so hard that they finally opened it, and I shouted in my broken English: "I not dog! I Sanni! I sleep inside!"[24]

In addition to a safe "home" the domestics received regular meals. Many farm girls who were used to hearty dinners, however, complained of the small portions served. They had to sneak extra food from the kitchen. Others went to a local Finnish restaurant on their afternoon off "and stuffed themselves with pancakes" so that for at least a day they would not go hungry.[25] One woman noted an ideological difference about eating and explained in a letter to her mother: "Canadians don't give enough food to anybody. They are afraid that if you eat too much you get sick and the Finns are afraid that if you don't eat enough you get sick."[26] Others complained of the miserly manner in which the mistress checked all food supplies. In one millionaire's home in Montreal, the maids were not allowed to have cream in their coffee. "When the lady asked for the hundredth time if there was cream in the coffee," explained one frustrated maid, "my friend took the entire cream pitcher and threw it against the wall." With a thoughtful sigh she added, "We Finns, you know, we have such temper—that *sisu*—has caused many a maid to lose her job."[27] On the other hand, many women were fed good balanced diets, were introduced to white bread, various vegetables and fruits unknown in their own country. Not only did they receive regular meals, they learned to "eat the Canadian way."

Living with a Canadian family they also learned to speak some English, usually enough to manage in the kitchen. Jokingly they described their language as *kitsi-Engelska*. Many were taught by their employers who found communication through a dictionary too cumbersome, others took language classes provided by the Finnish community during the "maid's day." The maids themselves realized the importance of learning the language:

> ...I am so thankful that right away I was placed in a job where there are only English-speaking people so that I just have to learn when I don't even hear anything else and here that is the main thing to learn to speak English first even when looking for work they don't ask if you know how to work but if you know the language of the country....[28]

Along with language skills, the maids were also given an immersion course on Canadian home appliances, customs and behaviour. On-the-job training included the introduction to vacuum cleaners, washing machines and the operations of gas ovens. The maids attentively observed the "ladies" and were soon acquiring new role models. In amazement Finnish men complained of the profusion of make-up used by the maids who had started to *playata laidia* (play the lady).[29] Women's clothing reflected the new image—hats, gloves and silk stockings being among the first items of purchase. Having obtained these symbols of Canadianization, the maids rushed to the photography studios and sent home pictures of themselves lounging on two-seater velvet sofas, sniffing at a rose and revealing strategically placed silk-stockinged legs. Other pictures showed women with huge hats, the likes of which could only be worn by the nobility or the minister's wife in Finland.[30] We can imagine what effect these photographs had on the relatives back home, or on the girlfriends still wearing tight scarves and wool stockings. Only one month in Canada, and the photographs showed a total transformation of a poor country woman into a sophisticated "lady" sipping tea from a silver pot, some needlepoint resting on her knee.

The reality, of course, was much different from the illusion created by the props in the photographers' studios. Undeniably, there were many advantages to being a live-in maid—an instant "home," on-the-job training and immersion in the country's language and customs. On the other hand, there were also serious complaints.

THE PROUD MAID

A recent study of domestic service in Canada blames the long working hours, hard work, lack of privacy and low status of domestic work for the unpopularity of the job.[31] The Finnish immigrant women certainly agreed with many of these complaints, but because of their cultural background, their position in the community and their special immigrant conditions, their view of domestic work was somewhat different.

Historians have suggested that for the young Irish girls in Boston domestic work actually represented upward mobility, since they had been unable to obtain any kind of work in Ireland. A study of Swedes in Chicago indicates that domestic work was reputable and accepted as the norm for the first-generation Swedish women who were almost exclusively working as maids.[32] This trend is evident among the Finnish domestics in Canada. When the community was so overwhelmingly composed of domestic servants, comparisons with other occupations became irrelevant. Instead the domestics created their own internal hierarchy. Their status came from a job well done and they took pride in their honesty, initiative and ability to work hard "to do what previously had taken two women."[33] Together they worked to create a sound collective image and to improve their working opportunities.

Within the social hierarchy of the domestics, those who specialized and worked for the "millionaires" had the highest status within the community.

Two Domestic servants in Toronto, 1915, posing in their new uniforms.

MHSO Collection, SR 6886 nr 13.

The salaries reflected the experience and the nature of the work, ranging from $15 a month before the First World War and during the twenties to as high as $50 a month. The cooks were at the top of the hierarchy and so too were nursemaids and companions. Chambermaids, kitchen helpers and "generals" followed, in that order.[34] For women with a Finnish cultural background, domestic service was not necessarily a "low status occupation." Furthermore, the maid's own view of her work and the community's response to it might indeed see it as reputable, well paid and even independent work.

Any deviance from this norm, any Finnish woman perceived as "lazy" or dishonest, was severely chastised in the Finnish-Canadian press for ruining the reputation of Finns as "most desirable and highly paid domestic servants."[35]

On an individual level, pride in their work – in their profession – is reflected in the comments of the domestics interviewed for this project. "My floors were the cleanest on the street," or "my laundry was out the earliest every morning" are typical of the self-congratulatory mood. Comparisons with other women were used to illustrate these points:

> Nobody had scrubbed that dirt off, did they look at me when I took off my only pair of shoes, got on my knees and scrubbed that muck till you could have eaten from the floor. Women weren't supposed to show their naked ankles, but heck, I wasn't about to ruin my shoes. Another Finlander, they thought![36]

They worked hard to gain the trust of their employers, and then they boasted, "If I said the sky was green, then the sky was green."[37] Finnish women often showed a strange mixture of an inferiority and superiority complex. While they might have respected the position of the "Missis," they often felt great distain for "her inability to do anything right." Helmi, who worked for a wealthy family in Sault Ste. Marie during the early twenties, is a prime example of the confidence and control that shines through from many of the stories told by domestics:

> When that Mrs. noticed that I could take care of all the cleaning, all the dishes and all the cooking, in fact, I ran the entire household, she became so lazy that she started to demand her breakfast in bed. Healthy woman! Just lying there and I had to carry the food to bed. Oh boy, that hurt the Finlander's *sisu* that a woman makes herself so shamefully helpless. What to do, what to come up with, when there

was no point to *kikkia* [kick back]. So I started making the most deli-
cious old-country pancakes, plenty of them and thick, and I added lots
of butter and whipped cream. Every morning I carried to the Mrs. a
huge plateful, and the Mrs. ate until she was as round as my pancakes.
The Mr. ordered her to go on a diet, and Helmi no longer had to take
breakfast to bed![38]

When Nellie McClung chose to make a Finnish domestic the heroine of her novel *Painted Fires*, she agreed with the image that Finnish
domestics had of themselves. Having had a Finnish maid, she was surprisingly familiar with their manners, pride, temper and customs. The
Finns, on the other hand, greeted the book with exalted praise as it
showed the Finnish maids "exactly as we like to think we are."[39] The
novel was promptly translated into Finnish and sold thousands of copies. The heroine, whose name was also Helmi, was honest to a fault,
loyal, extremely clean and hard working. She was also strong, stubborn and defiant. For example, in one scene Helmi slams the dishtray
on the head of another domestic who had not pre-rinsed the greasy
plates. In the ensuing chaos the employer asks, "Isn't that kind of behaviour so typical of the Finns, Maggie! They are clean, swift, but so
hot-headed."[40]

McClung's stereotype of a spirited Finnish domestic finds many
counterparts in the literary tradition of Finland and of Finns in North
America. Because of the Finnish women's love of theatre, of acting
and performing, they were often in the position to choose and even
write plays for the stage. Invariably the maid was portrayed as "intelli-
gent and honest," constantly involved in her self-improvement while
the masters were corrupt, lazy and often stupid. In the Finnish-Canadian
socialist literature, the class struggle is depicted through scenes of supe-
rior servants suffering under less capable masters. The beloved poems
of Aku Päiviö, the best known Finnish-Canadian socialist writer, reinforced the superiority of the victim. One woman confided: "Every time
I read the poem 'Woman's Day', I just cried. It was so true that I could
feel it in my bones. The book, you know, was censored by the government, so I removed a tile from the kitchen floor and hid it. When I

was in the kitchen by myself, early in the morning, I would read the poem over and over again. It was my private source of strength."[41]

Another woman, Sanni, describes the Finnish domestics by taking examples from the writings of Minna Canth and Juhani Tervapää. The latter's play *Juurakon Hulda* (Hulda from the Stump District) gave Sanni her inspiration and role model. Hulda was a poor farm girl who took employment as a domestic servant, but through hard work and persistent studying in the middle of the night, she eventually outshone her employers with her wit, intelligence and honesty.[42] "You might be a servant," said Sanni, "but it doesn't mean you are dumb":

> When you can read, a whole new world opens up for you. It doesn't matter where you live, how far from the civilization, or in what poverty. Once I got started, I read everything I could get my hands on...Finnish women are like that Juurakon Hulda, they come from such poor circumstances with nothing in their name, but through hard work and self-education they try to get ahead, find dignity, learn to see beyond their own neighbourhood.[43]

Of course, not all Finnish domestics fit this collective image. Many a woman quietly cried herself to sleep, "too tired to get up to get a handkerchief."[44] The image, however, did create a role model of a domestic that Finnish women ought to emulate, and if they reached this goal, if they convinced their friends and the community that they had earned the respect of their employers, they also gained the support and respect of the community. A maid who was not afraid to take the household reins into her hands had high status in her community. Many bizarre stories emerge when women explain that really they were the ones in control in such families as the Molsons, Otises and Masseys. Perhaps the most outrageous comes from a woman who served the widow of a Governor General in Quebec. She discovered that her living quarters on the first floor of the house were infested with rats. Having spent one entire night catching them, she laid the seven fat specimens on the breakfast table.[45]

Laundry day. MHSO MSR 10971-11.

"WHEN YOU ARE A DOMESTIC YOU ARE NOTHING BUT A SLAVE"

While the generally perceived low status of domestic work was not a serious deterrent to the Finnish immigrant women, the demand for submissiveness was almost impossible for Finns to meet. The most serious and persistent complaints came from those domestics who bemoaned their lack of privacy, their loss of individuality, their sense of being totally controlled by a strange family. Domestics who stayed with the same family for a long period of time lost their chance to have a family of their own. Children and husbands were seldom tolerated by the employers. Those lucky couples who were able to hire themselves out as butler-maid teams were rare exceptions.[46] Not many husbands were satisfied to have a part-time wife who was available only every other Sunday and one afternoon a week, although such "hidden" marriages did exist. More often, the maid became an extension of somebody else's family and an integral part of the daily routines, but not necessarily any part of the emotional life. As years went by and the maid aged, the chance of ever having a family of her own became an impossible dream. The exceptionally high age of the women giving birth in Montreal to illegitimate children—37.6 in 1936-39—suggests that some women made a deliberate decision to have a child of their own while it was still physically possible.[47]

A Finnish pastor of the Montreal congregation during the late seventies regretted the fate of some of his parishioners, most of whom were women who had worked as live-in domestics in Montreal during the twenties and thirties, and now were totally alone.[48] The families did not provide pensions, nor take much interest in the whereabouts of a retired maid. To make matters worse, the maid had no family, no home, no life of her own. "All my life, I just worked and worked, I seldom went anywhere or met anybody," remembers one resident of a Vancouver old-age home, "and now I know nobody, I am just wondering why God keeps me alive?"[49] The tremendous personal sacrifices demanded from a reliable domestic, the willingness to become a shadow, a quiet figure in the corner tending to the household tasks, was described by one maid as "equal to being buried alive."[50]

This sad fate fell on some Finnish domestics, but many others vigorously fought against it. The free time, the precious Wednesday or Thursday afternoon off, when the maid was allowed to exercise her own will, to be a decision-making person and to meet people of her

4848 Varpu Lindström

choice, was carefully planned in advance. Here the Finnish community was of special help and support.

COMMUNITY SUPPORT

The Finnish communities quickly adjusted to the maid's unusual time schedules in order to have some social activity. Finnish organizations, which until the thirties were largely socialist locals of the Finnish Organization of Canada (FOC), scheduled their social occasions, gymnastics practices, theatre rehearsals and dances during "the maid's day." The halls kept their doors open so that the maids could relax after their weekly pilgrimage to Eaton's. They could go and have coffee, meet each other, discuss the work situation, find out about new job opportunities and for a few brief hours escape from their employers. The FOC locals were not the only groups vying for the maid's attention. Finnish congregations, especially in Toronto and Montreal, also catered to them, scheduling their services for Wednesday and Sunday evenings and providing social coffees and reading-rooms for the maids.

When the Finnish consul of Canada, Akseli Rauanheimo, tried to convince Canadian industries, railroads and the government to contribute to the building of a Finnish immigrant home in Montreal, one of his chief concerns was the welfare of the maids. "Many of them have nothing to do on their afternoons off except sit alone on park benches." The home was not only to be used for entertainment, it could also function as a refuge for those women who were mistreated by their employers and who had no other "home" to go to then.[51] Similarly, such temporary shelters for maids in other major communities were usually provided by those women who ran the maids' employment services.[52] Thus, the Finnish domestics could have a sense of belonging to a community, they could share their work experiences with other domestics, and they knew that if their conditions became intolerable other options were open—they could quit and leave and know that they didn't have to spend the night on the street.

This added to the bargaining power of the Finnish domestics who knew that their services were in demand and who had the means to contact new employers. Most Finnish maids did take advantage of their ability "to slam the door so that the chandeliers were shaking," or alternately to "sneak out of the backdoor so that nobody would notice." During their first year as domestics in Canada, the women changed jobs frequently. For example, the Finnish Immigrant Home in Montreal accommodated women who were changing their jobs for the sixth time within a year.[53] Similarly the biographies and interviews concur that at first women took almost any work and then shopped around until a suitable family came along.

The Finnish employment agencies were the key to the domestic's flexibility. They were quick to advise the women not to accept intolerable conditions. Many enterprising women kept rooms for just such a purpose, and there is every indication that they kept close watch on the "greenhorns" who were most vulnerable to exploitation. Still, even with a helpful Finnish woman, the hiring was a harrowing experience. Elli remembered it vividly:

> The first lady who came picked me because I was obviously the cheapest and strongest one, she wanted a greenhorn who would work like a dog... I cried and washed her floors and I was always hungry, but I stayed there for four months until I went back to Mrs. Engman.... She got me a new job right away, but this time I quit after one crazy day, sneaked out secretly.... In my third place I stayed for seven and a half months and was able to demand $35.00 a month, but I quit that place too... because I had to be home at eleven o'clock and it broke my heart to leave the dances during the intermission and see my good-looking boyfriend stay behind.[54]

As the maids gained confidence in their own ability to work, they became more defiant in the work place and often refused to be treated like slaves. Hilja explained:

> In one place where I worked the lady started to shout at me because I hadn't got up early enough to do the washing at 6:00 A.M. I told her that nobody shouts at me and I quit. I decided to take that day off and went to stay at Ilomaki's [home for maids], but as soon as I got there the phone rang for me. It was the employment office calling, they fig-

ured that I had quit because my lady had called for a new maid. They phoned me to let me know that a new job was already waiting for me. Next day I was working again.[55]

Finnish women peeling potatoes for Hoito Restaurant in Thunder Bay.

MHSO MSR 6891, part 1 Nr 10.

In addition to the private agencies which received payment for every maid they placed, the Finnish Immigrant Home and many churches arranged for employment for the maids. The system was the same kind of "cattle auction." Ida remembers that "the women just stood in a line and the ladies came to pick which one they wanted."[56] While most Finnish-Canadian sources claim that the Finnish maids were sought-after workers, there are also examples to the contrary: "There were places that would take only Finns, but there were also places that wouldn't take a Finn for any money. Once I was told bluntly that 'We won't hire Finns, because they are all red and stubborn.'"[57]

One woman remembers being told to quit singing the "International" while washing the kitchen floor. "I'll sing what I want," she replied and with that lost her job.[58] Nellie McClung also referred to the reputation of Finnish maids as socialists and trouble-makers.[59] But on the whole the employers were not interested in the private lives of their maids, not to speak of their political opinions, as long as the floors were scrubbed, the laundry washed and the family fed. Edna Ferber vividly describes the family's ignorance of the maid's private world in her short story of a Finnish maid in the United States.[60]

THE CLASS-CONSCIOUS MAID

To some Finnish domestics, the availability of work and the supportive networks within the community were not enough. Instead they sought a more elusive goal—a strong collective spirit.

Class consciousness, unlike such characteristics as temper or shyness, is acquired through experience, cultivated by self-study and cemented by daily injustices. Finland was swept by a socialist fervour during the first two decades of the nineteenth century and the question of maids was hotly debated in both the legislature and media. Special homes for maids were established where women could acquire domestic skills. A newspaper, *Palvelijatar* (Maid), discussed at length "maid's rights" and suggested protective measures. The paper's editor, Miina Sillanpää, a Social Democratic member of Parliament since 1907, raised the grievances in the Finnish legislature.[61] Thus it is highly possible that many maids who arrived in North America had already learnt to accept the socialist world-view in Finland.

Because domestic service was the major occupation for Finnish women, it received much attention from the Finnish socialists in North America. The socialist leaders were worried that the live-in domestics would adopt the "capitalist outlook of their employers when they are clearly an indistinguishable part of the working class."[62] They were baffled as to how to organize the domestics who were serving thousands of different "bosses" all over Canada. In the end, the main impetus was placed on raising the individual consciousness, making each maid fight for her own rights within her particular place of employment, while the community would provide her with the best possible support: knowledge, training, cooperative housing and minimum guide-lines for wages and working hours. Unsuccessful efforts at unionizing the maids were also made in major urban areas.

The key to bringing the maids into the socialist fold was to give them hope of improved working conditions by frankly discussing the problems and solutions through the Finnish North American press. In this the socialist women's newspaper, *Toveritar*, which had over 3,000 subscribers in Canada in 1929, played a vital role.[63] In a special issue for the maids, on 9 May 1916, the editor, Selma Jokela-McClone, analyzed the situation:

1. While the factory worker is seldom in direct contact with her employer, the maid has personally to face her boss on a daily basis and negotiate her undefined work.

2. A maid is a highly skilled worker, yet she has no possibility to learn her trade before she starts working.

3. Maids do not necessarily work for the big capitalists, many serve the middle class and even the more prosperous working class, which can confuse the issue of class struggle.

To deal with these problems Jokela-McClone suggested that:

1. Because the maid meets her employer as a human being she must have the self-confidence and the sense of self-worth to demand decent human treatment.

2. Maids must become professionals by improving their skills to the utmost of their ability. The key to successful bargaining is the ability to perform well.

3. They must organize maids' clubs, cooperative homes, employment exchanges and raise the class-consciousness of the maids before they can put forth strong demands.[64]

These guide-lines were adopted by Finnish socialist women's groups in Canada, but not without debate. Many questioned "the need for special skills," or the argument that a maid was a professional, or a highly trained worker. There were those who saw the maid as "an appendix to the parasite class" and not a trustworthy member of the working class. Maids themselves asked what good would training centres or clubs do when the maids didn't have the free time to attend them. Despite the skepticism, attempts were made to implement the plan.[65]

In New York and San Francisco well-organized and highly effective maids' cooperative homes were established. These were seen as a model for other communities to emulate. In Canada the cooperative maids' home movement among the Finns had sporadic support at best. The need for such homes in Canada was partially met by private establishments which provided temporary housing when necessary. The employment exchange for Finnish maids was also in the hands of Finnish women who were generally trusted and reliable, unlike the situation in Manhattan, for example, where several large American agencies "competed for the Finnish maids."[66] Besides, in 1916, both the United States and Canada were experiencing shortages of domestic servants, "giving the maids great opportunities to be selective." In 1922 an article in *Vapaus* concluded that obtaining work was the least of the maids' problems, but rather the inhumanly long working days.[67]

By the mid-1920s, when socialist activity among the Finns had taken a more radical turn toward communism, the question of maids' unions and organizations rose again. This time, the response was at least lukewarm. The first Palvelijatar Yhdistys (Maids' Organization) was founded in Toronto on 6 December 1925.[68] Prior to this the Finnish Organization of Canada's Toronto local had given their Don Hall free of charge for the maids to use on their afternoon off. In 1926 the organization placed a permanent advertisement in the *Telegram* and set up a job exchange at the hall. Later the advertisement was only placed in the paper if someone was in need of work. At times the organization had over twenty paying members and then it seemed to "go to sleep." The last time it was "woken up" was on 6 January 1929, under the name of "Finnish Domestic Club."[69] A year earlier the Chinese community of Toronto had established a union of domestic workers at 87 Elizabeth Street complete with an employment exchange. Among the Finns a cooperative home for the maids was discussed, but it never materialized.

In 1927, Vancouver women also decided to establish a cooperative home and employment exchange for the maids. They set up a fund for this purpose, but by the end of 1928 they gave up the idea. Instead, they decided to investigate the possibility of joining the existing Domestic Servant's Union, mainly made up of Chinese domestics. Nothing came of this joint venture.[70]

The largest Finnish maids' organization was established in Montreal, where the need for protection was the greatest since the city was the immediate recipient of all the newly arrived maids coming off the transatlantic steamers. Here a cooperative home was not only discussed but also established in 1930, only to be dissolved within two years by the depression. This home and job exchange was in competition with the Finnish Immigrant Home established by the Consul of Finland and the Seamen's Mission in 1927. From the beginning the housing co-op had over thirty members.[71] In 1928 an article in *Vapaus* pointed out that the city had about 500 Finnish women of whom less than 2 percent were housewives; the rest were all working as maids or in the service industries. A newly arrived maid might only receive a wage of $20 a month, and the only weapon used by Finnish women to improve their working conditions was to change jobs constantly in search of a better employer.[72] The maids' organization was founded in September 1928 and was quite active. The success of actually getting a cooperative home off the ground was not unbiased because: "so many of the women who joined up were former members of workers' organizations and unions in Finland and thus, right from the beginning we were able to have experienced, capable women to carry on the cause."[73]

Similar maids' groups were established in Sudbury in 1928, in Sault Ste. Marie in 1929 and more sporadically in Port Arthur and Timmins during 1928-30. Common to all these maids' organizations was the desire to achieve minimum wage levels. The women in Sault Ste. Marie all swore that they would not "scab" for lower wages.[74] In Sudbury the maids were keen to establish insurance schemes for the sick and unemployed.[75] In all locations great emphasis was placed on self-education, not in domestic skills, but in class-consciousness and in understanding the role of women in a communist society.

In total, a rough estimate would suggest that about 200 Finnish domestics belonged to the organizations designed for the specific purpose of promoting maids' interests. The small numbers suggest that domestic servants did not have the time or will to give their only afternoon off for meetings, especially since other Finnish women's groups could carry on the task. In northern Ontario the Timmins domestics suggested total integration of women's organizations instead of splintering women into small interest groups.[76] Finnish men "did not take the organizations seriously," and the groups were not strong enough to have any concrete impact on wages. "Despite this," concludes a published assessment of the maids' organizations, they had great impact in making the maids realize that they too were part of the working class and most welcome in socialist circles."[77]

> No matter how good the family you work in, when you are a maid, you are nothing but a slave. I won't be a slave![78]

Domestic service, the greatest employer of Finnish women, clearly had many problems such as long hours, hard work and lack of privacy. Still, it continued to attract Finnish women, at least initially, because of the perceived advantages of room and board and learning the language and customs of the employers. It was also work that Finnish women were able and accustomed to doing, and the pay was sufficient to meet their immediate demands. Women could see considerable upward mobility within the hierarchy of domestic service and could conceivably double their wages within a year. The stigma of low status work was not very relevant in the Finnish community where most women were, or had been, domestics. Furthermore, the number of Finnish maids in the urban centres was great enough to force the community to set up their activities around the maids' schedules, thus lessening the pain of isolation.

While the Finnish communities could claim that many of their maids were class-conscious workers, they did not succeed in establishing long-term unions or cooperative homes. Still, by collectively keeping up their good image, Finnish domestics were some of the highest paid in the country. The more informal arrangements of maids' meeting-rooms, employment exchanges and private "homes" increased the flexibility of the Finnish domestics and gave them greater bargaining power with the employers. Yet domestic service demanded great personal sacrifices which most women were unwilling to make. As soon as other opportunities presented themselves, Finnish maids left their live-in situations and tried to find more independent work.

This award-winning article was first published in Jean Burnet (ed.) Looking into My Sister's Eyes: an Exploration in Women's History, *The Multicultural History Society of Ontario, 1986. It has been republished with permission of the publisher.*

ENDNOTES

[1] *Vapaus*, 30 May 1922, signed by Adolf Leaf.

[2] Ramsey Cook and Wendy Mitchinson, eds., *The Proper Sphere: Woman's Place in Canadian Society* (Toronto, 1976), pp. 172–74.

[3] Marilyn J. Barber, "Below Stairs: The Domestic Servant," *Material History Bulletin*, No. 19 (Ottawa, 1984); Marilyn Barber, "The Women Ontario Welcomed: Immigrant Domestics for Ontario Homes, 1870-1930," *Ontario History*, vol. LXXII, no. 3 (September 1980).

[4] Joy Parr, *Labouring Children* (London, 1980); Kenneth Bagnell, *Little Immigrants* (Toronto, 1980); Gail H. Corbett, *Barnado Children in Canada* (Woodview, Ont., 1981).

[5] Makeda Silvera, *Silenced* (Toronto, 1983).

[6] Ibid., pp. 11–40; Genevieve Leslie, "Domestic Service in Canada, 1880-1920," in Janice Acton, Penny Goldsmith and Bonnie Shepard, eds., *Women at Work* (Canadian Women's Educational Press, 1974), pp. 71–125; in 1985 live-in domestic servants are allowed to enter Canada without immigrant status as temporary foreign workers.

[7] "Emigration from Finland 1893–1944," New Canadian Immigration Regulations concerning emigration from Scandinavia and Finland, RG 76 vol. 651 C 4682, Public Archives of Canada.

[8] *Toveritar,* 10 February 1925, poem by Arvo Lindewall.

[9] Leslie, "Domestic Service in Canada," Table A, p. 72.

[10] Barber, "Below Stairs," p. 38.

[11] The term in Finnish is *piikomaan Amerikkaan.*

[12] Dominion of Canada, Report of the Department of Immigration and Colonization for the Fiscal Year ended March 31, 1929.

[13] "Finnish Immigrant Home Records", MG 28 V128 Vol. 1 File 1.

[14] For Montreal figures, see Varpu Lindström-Best, "Finnish Immigrants and the Depression: A Case Study of Montreal," Ph.D. II paper (York University, 1981) and for information on Toronto, see her "Tailor-Maid: the Finnish Immigrant Community of Toronto before the First World War," in Robert F. Harney, ed., *Gathering Place: Peoples and Neighbourhoods of Toronto, 1834–1945* (MHSO, 1985).

[15] Interviews with Martta Norlen and Mary Syrjälä, Winnipeg, 1983.

[16] Census of Canada, 1911, Volume VI, Table I, "Occupations of the people compared for all of Canada."

[17] Interview with Tyyne Pihlajamäki, Timmins, 1982.

[18] Interview with Rolph Koskinen, Parry Sound, 1983.

[19] Interview with Helen Tarvainen, Toronto, 1978; see also Joan Sangster, "Finnish Women in Ontario, 1890-1930," *Polyphony,* vol. 3, no. 2 (Fall 1981).

[20] American Letter Collection, LOIM: IV Letter from Aino Kuparinen, a maid who came to Toronto in 1924.

[21] Interview with Lahja Söderberg, Vancouver, 1983.

[22] "Scandinavian and Finnish Domestics," RG 76 Vol. 436 File 654504.

[23] Interview with Martta Kujanpää, Toronto, 1978.

[24] Interview with Sanni Salmijärvi, Thunder Bay, 1984.

[25] Interview with Martta Norlen, Winnipeg, 1983.

[26] American Letter Collection, EURA: XXI Letter from Aino Norkooli who immigrated to Fort William, Ontario in 1923.

[27] Taped recording of Ida Toivonen's reminiscences in Thunder Bay, 1983 and her handwritten notes. York University Archives, Varpu Lindström Collection.

[28] American Letter Collection, KAR: CXXVI Letter from Sylvia Hakola in Schreiber, Ontario dated 26.09.1926.

[29] Carl Ross, "Finnish American Women in Transition, 1910–1920," in Michael G. Karni, ed., Finnish Diaspora II: United States (MHSO, 1981).

[30] For example see Varpu Lindström-Best and Charles M. Sutyla, Terveisiä Ruusa-tädiltä: Kanadan suomalaisten ensimmäinen sukupolvi (Helsinki, 1984), especially the chapter on "Valokuvaajalla" (At the Photographers), pp. 143–56.

[31] Leslie, "Domestic Work in Canada," p. 85; Toveritar, 20 June 1916, an article explaining why women do not like to be domestic servants.

[32] Ulf Beijbom, Swedes in Chicago, Studia Historica Upsaliensia XXXVIII, especially pp. 197–98.

[33] "Consulate of Finland Correspondence," MG8 G62 Vol. 2, File 59.

[34] Interview with Rolph Koskinen, Parry Sound, 1983.

[35] Interview with Hilja Sihvola, Parry Sound, 1983.

[36] Ida Toivonen Recordings, Thunder Bay, 1983.

[37] Interview with Lahja Söderberg, Vancouver, 1983.

[38] Interview with Helmi Vanhatalo, Sault Ste. Marie, 1981.

[39] Nellie L. McClung, Painted Fires, was translated into Finnish by Väinö Nyman, Suomalaistyttö Amerikassa (Helsinki, 1926).

[40] Copies of related correspondence courtesy of J. Donald Wilson.

[41] Aku Päiviö poem "Naisten Päivä."

[42] Juhani Tervapää, (Hella Wuolajoki) Juurakon Hulda (Helsinki, 1937).

[43] Interview with Sanni Salmijärvi, Thunder Bay, 1984.

[44] Interview with Saimi Ranta, Niagara Falls, 1974.

[45] Ida Toivonen Recordings, Thunder Bay, 1983.

[46] Butler-maid, cook-chauffeur, etc., combinations were especially popular during the depression when men could not obtain any other kind of work.

[47] "St. Michael's Finnish Ev. Lutheran Church," Province of Quebec Registration of a Live Birth, MG 8 G62 Vol. 7, Files 23-25.

[48] Discussions with Rev. Markku Suokonautio, Montreal, 1979.

[49] Interview with Impi Lehto, Toronto, 1974.

[50] Interview with Martta Huhtala, Waubamik, Ontario, 1983.

[51] "Consulate of Finland Correspondence," MG8 G62 Vol. 2 File 59.

[52] In Toronto alone, there were at least twelve women who took in maids and found them jobs on a more or less permanent basis.

[53] Immigrant Home Registers for Women list a total of 3,044 women between 1927 and 1931, MG 28 V128 Vol. 6 Files 1–3.

[54] Interview with Elli Mäki, Parry Sound, 1984.

[55] Interview with Hilja Sihvola, Parry Sound, 1983.

[56] Ida Toivonen Recordings.

[57] Ibid.

[58] Interview with Sanni Salmijärvi, Thunder Bay, 1984.

[59] McClung, Painted Fires; the heroine is often confused in the novel with a socialist Finnish woman who has the same last name but a reputation as a trouble-maker.

[60] Edna Ferber, *Every Other Thursday*, a short story about the life of a Finnish Domestic in New York City.

[61] Oma Mäkikossa, *Yhteiskunnalle omistettu elämä: Miina Sillanpään elämän ja työn vaiheita* (Helsinki, 1947).

[62] *Toveritar*, 18 January 1916.

[63] *Toveritar*, 9 May 1916; see also Varpu Lindström-Best and Allen Seager, *"Toveritar* and the Finnish Canadian Women's Movement 1900–1930," a paper presented in Frankfurt, West Germany, February 12–15, 1985.

[64] *Toveritar*, 9 May 1916.

[65] *Toveritar*, 6 June 1916.

[66] Ross, "Finnish American Women," pp. 239-55.

[67] *Vapaus* article, "Nais palvelijain asema Kanadassa" (The position of female domestics in Canada) was also printed in *Toveritar*, 30 May 1922.

[68] *Vapaus*, 6 December 1925.

[69] *Vapaus*, 18 January 1926; 26 January 1926; 28 December 1926; 18 January 1927; 29 January 1929.

[70] *Vapaus*, 19 June 1926; 07 June 1927; 05 June 1928; 12 February 1929; the organization stopped earlier on 13 December 1928.

[71] "Finnish Organization of Canada Correspondence with Montreal," MG 28 V46 Vol. 11 File 7.

[72] *Vapaus*, 15 August 1928.

[73] *Vapaus*, 24 September 1928.

[74] *Vapaus*, 01 October, 1929.

[75] *Vapaus*, 29 January 1929.

[76] *Vapaus*, 18 March 1930.

[77] *Vapaus*, 20 December 1929.

[78] Interview with Sanni Salmijärvi, Thunder Bay, 1984.

The Radicalization of Finnish Farm Women in Northwestern Ontario

"My Mother was radicalized by anger, she was so upset with the
hard work and isolation, how women were treated, and the
social injustices foreigners faced. And then she read the socialist
newspapers and listened to the speakers, that's how she became a radical.
I did not take on the radical politics and the activist role voluntarily.
It was my mother's will, and I did not dare to oppose her, not ever.
I do support the working class and work for social justice."

Thus Taimi (Pitkänen) Davis described her immigrant, socialist mother Kirsti (Korhonen), and her own relationship to radical politics. One does not immediately think of a remote rural village in northwestern Ontario as an ideal breeding ground for a socialist world view. Female subsistence farmers are neither wage workers nor housewives. Their problems and concerns often fall between the cracks in the mainstream socialist debate and in women's history in general.[1] Nor does one expect that poverty-stricken students from a one-room rural school in Canada would travel to Moscow to study Marxism or that subsistence farmers would spend so much effort in educating their children to be radical leaders. But a group of Finnish women in Kivikoski, in northwestern Ontario, did become radicalized and attempted to recruit their children into the socialist, and later, communist movement.

The story of Kirsti Pitkänen and her daughter, Taimi Davis, shows the hardships and isolation rural women faced and the work and social activities they performed. It also reveals the often difficult relationship between an immigrant mother and her Canadian-born daughter. It portrays the challenges some women posed to their gender boundaries and the "dreams of equality" they shared during the 1920s and 1930s. The example of parents, the community, and radical female role models were of paramount importance in the process of making radical activists of these second generation Finnish immigrants. This immigrant mother, restricted by language and cultural barriers, was unable to realize her dream of active participation in building a socialist society beyond her own ethnic community. Having recognized this fact, she tried to shift this heavy responsibility on to her Canadian-born daughter's shoulders. Although not recounting a typical Canadian immigration story, this case study offers a glimpse of the process of radicalization in one specific, if unlikely, community. It offers a new grassroots perspective to rural women's radical politics, placing the phenomenon in the context of family, immigrant culture, class, and gender role expectations at the time. A case study of this small community, focused on one family, gives a human face to the often ignored history of rural, immigrant women. It also gives voice to women who could not speak English and whose lives have not been deemed worthy of historical study.

HISTORIOGRAPHY

During the 1980s and 1990s, several scholars published studies of the history of women on Canadian left. Linda Kealey's *Enlisting Women for the Cause: Women, Labour, and the Left in Canada, 1890–1920* explores the early participation of women in socialist politics and left-wing organizations. Kealey's comprehensive study, which includes radical immigrant women and their ethnic organizations, aims to rectify the lack of attention paid to labour and socialist women. She argues that Canadian labour and socialist movements benefited from the invaluable input of women as organizers, fundraisers, and as political leaders. Kealey encourages a wider focus that also includes women's activism in the home, the neighbourhood, and the community, as well as in the union, the party, or the workplace. One of her recurrent themes is the supportive and less valued roles women played in the socialist movement.[2] Janice Newton's *The Feminist Challenge to the Canadian Left, 1900–1918* concentrates on English-speaking socialist women and the discourse around the "woman question." It focuses on activists and working-class women. Joan Sangster's book, *Dreams of Equality: Women on the Canadian Left, 1920–1950*, offers a powerful analysis of how women's issues were dealt with on the political left, especially within the Communist Party of Canada and the Co-operative Commonwealth Federation (CCF).

These books, together with a number of studies that explore the participation of the Finnish and Ukrainian communities in left-wing politics, provide a critical and comprehensive foundation for the analysis of Canada's radical women. They depict the solidarity that occasionally existed among women on the left, but they also reveal discrimination and ethnocentric values that sometimes pitted English women against immigrant women. They argue that socialist ideals and the reality of women's lives are in conflict and that patriarchal structures impede women's activism.[3]

Both Kealey and Sangster point out the absence of information and records on lesser known activists and "ordinary" women in the radical movement. While making an important contribution to the understanding of women's roles in left-wing politics and their contributions to the labour movement, the existing studies pay little attention to non-English speaking rural women or the impact of radicalism on the relationships between immigrant mothers and their Canadian-born daughters. Sangster laments the fact that many Communist Party of Canada records relevant to the role of women in the movement have been destroyed. The few biographies written about Canadian women on the left are, according to her, "incomplete and hagiographical."[4] The very diversity of the women who were involved in the Canadian labour movement poses an additional challenge to historians. In the absence of readily available documents, a case study based on primary research—letters, photographs, and oral interviews—can bring new in sights to the study of "ordinary women" in Canadian left-wing politics. Most of my earlier research has focused on Finnish women's wage work. I have placed special emphasis on the lives of domestics, women in the service industry, lumber-camp women, and Finnish women in the war industry.[5] While some research has been done on Finnish Prairie farmers, the struggles of subsistence farm women in northern Ontario have not been studied.[6] Recently, Finnish women in Canada have published some autobiographical accounts, but these narratives are devoid of political content and none depict the life of women on the left.[7]

Taimi (Pitkänen) Davis's political orientation is clear; she is a lifelong member of the Communist Party of Canada. My article is based on interviews with Davis and an examination of her private collection of personal documents. Women's history, especially when it relies on oral history, photographs, and memoirs, has been the subject of intense debate among feminist historians. Many scholars have asked critical questions about the subjectivity of both the author and her sources. In this article, I have applied feminist methodology by involving Taimi Davis in the entire process of research: she has participated in interviews, reviewed transcripts, and assisted in the creation of the final product. Davis was not only an interviewee but also a partner in formulating the research questions.[8]

IMMIGRATION FROM FINLAND TO NORTHERN ONTARIO.

In 1896, when Canada'a minister of the interior, Clifford Sifton, began his active recruitment of immigrants from Europe, his agents did not overlook Finland. Although looking ostensibly for farmers, the immigration officials recognized that Finns could also be employed in railroad construction and in the mines and forests of Canada's north. Bythe turn of the century, small Finnish communities had clustered around the coal mines of British Columbia and in northern and northwestern Ontario. Some men had been able to obtain free land on the prairies.

Varpu Lindström, author and Taimi Davis, interviewee

Community building, however, did not start in earnest until a significant number of women also arrived. Most of the women who came
were single and found employment in the service industries. The majority of the Finnish immigrants came from rural areas, especially the

western, coastal regions of Ostrobothnia. They were usually the "surplus" sons and daughters of peasants or children of landless agricultural workers and had come to Canada in search of better economic opportunities. These Finnish immigrants, both male and female, had attended at least some school and were almost universally literate.[9]

Port Arthur-Fort William, Ontario, (now named Thunder Bay) boasted one of the first and largest concentrations of Finns in Canada. In 1882, 11 Finnish women were reported in the area and, by the turn of the century, their number had risen to about 200. By 1907, Port Arthur had Finnish businesses, rooming houses, restaurants, bootlegging operations, grocery stores, bakeries, and butcher shops. Finns had constructed churches and socialist halls that provided a wide range of spiritual, social, cultural and political activities. In 1907, *Työkansa* (Working People), a socialist Finnish-language newspaper was launched in Port Arthur. Thus, in the first decade of the twentieth century, Port Arthur already had a thriving Finntown. Indeed, the town's reputation had spread to many villages back in Finland, and soon the city became the most popular first destination for newly arrived immigrants. About 30 per cent of the 5,400 Finns living in Canada in 1911 resided in northwestern Ontario, and they made up nearly 10 per cent of the population of Port Arthur.[10]

Encouraged by the availability of forested land near Port Arthur and Fort William, many Finnish men (women did not qualify for free land) acquired homesteads within a 50-kilometre radius of the city. Around 1900, Finns began to clear the northern Ontario bush in earnest and to establish rural settlements such as Intola (Place of Enthusiasm), Tarmola (Place of Vigour), Toimela (Place of Activity), Lappe (Lappi or Lapland), Suomi (Finland), North Branch, Sunshine, Nolalu, Alppila (Place of Alps), and Kivikoski (Stone Rapids).[11]

The influx of so many Finns to the area was not part of any official plan of block settlement but rather rose from the immigrants' desire to settle near each other and from information that travelled by word-of-mouth and letters to the old country. Finns thought farming a good insurance against starvation during periods of unemployment and that the forests could be converted into the farmer's first cash crop. They were keen to take advantage of the 160-acre parcels of land that were available for a dollar. A stunned government employee remembered that in one day, in 1901, over 100 "Finlanders," men, women and children, came to his office to apply for land in Lybster township.[12] This mass movement of Finns to rural Thunder Bay created pockets of rural settlement that were almost exclusively Finnish.

KIVIKOSKI SETTLEMENT

By 1911, Kivikoski, a community located in the townships of McIntyre and Gorham and situated 12 to 15 kilometres northwest of Port Arthur, included about 60 inhabitants. Most residents grew potatoes and other root crops for personal consumption and kept some cows, pigs, and chickens. The community was, by 1911, sufficiently organized to have a post office and to plan for the construction of a one-room log schoolhouse. With one exception, all of the residents of Kivikoski, including the teacher, Hannah Rissanen, and her 15 students were immigrants of Finnish origin.[13]

The turn-of-the-century settlers from Finland who came to tame the northwestern Ontario wilderness were quite accustomed to hardships, cold climates, virgin forests, and fields filled with stones. Finnish immigrants, both male and female, were used to hard work and had learned to eke out a living from northern subsistence farms by augmenting their food supplies with fishing, hunting, and trapping. What they did not anticipate before migrating was the social and physical isolation they would experience in Canada. Neighbours were far away and roads, where they existed, were often impassable. Yet the most significant barrier of all was the immigrants' inability to communicate with the wider community. All official business outside the rural settlement had to be conducted in English, and they spoke only Finnish and, sometimes, Swedish. The social and physical isolation was hardest on women, especially if they had young children; they would be chained to the homesteads for months, sometimes years, at a time. Women clung to their family, closest neighbours, and community for support, hoping that at least their children, fluent in English and in the customs of the land, could break through the invisible barriers. In this respect, the experience of Finnish rural women was not different from many other immigrant women in Canada. Unlike the quaint, conservative, and pious rural communities depicted in Canadian school books produced at the turn of the century, Kivikoski never established a church. No religious Sunday school, no church picnics, and no stern sermons brought the community together. The neighbouring communities to the east and west of Kivikoski—Tarmola, North Branch, Intola, and Alppila—also lacked a place of worship. The only Finnish rural congregation in the area was a Lutheran church in Lappe, north of Kivikoski, and its pastor occasionally visited one family in Kivikoski and another family sometimes attended the church. Local histories refer to the "paucity of church activity" and to the fact that Kivikoski was "predominantly left-wing in its sentiments."[14] Kivikoski residents filled their lives with hard work. Social and political activities gave meaning to the little free time they allowed themselves. These activities centered on the school, which, until 1921, also served as the socialist community hall. Soon after the school opened, it received a shipment of books from Port Arthur that formed the basis for a "rural Finnish farmer's library."[15] The books included fiction, farming guides, and political, especially Marxist, texts in the Finnish language.

WOMEN AND WORK ON SUBSISTENCE FARMS

Women's work on subsistence farms was arduous and never ending. The ladies daintily sipping tea from fine china depicted in the Government of Canada's recruitment literature or the finely dressed damsels on the pages of Eaton's catalogue had no counterparts in Kivikoski. The reality in the "Land of Opportunity" or the "Land of the Second Chance," as the propaganda booklets the Canadian Government distributed in Finland were entitled, was very different indeed. Taimi's account of her mother's work reveals the strict gender division of labour that existed on the farm and recalls all farm women's battles against social isolation and perceived injustices.

Taimi explained: "In Finnish homes only women did the milking and barn work. I never knew a Finnish man who looked after the children or the barn. If women had small children, one after the other, there was no chance to go visiting or to go to town. Winter or summer women could not go beyond the barn and even that was perilous. With one or two children mothers could put the little ones in a stall while milking, feeding, and shovelling dung. Some women did not go to town for years. They never had a holiday, never a sleep-in; day after day they lifted heavy items, milk cans, 100 pound sacks of feed, carried in pails of water and helped men in all other heavy work as well. Women did almost everything and were always taken for granted."

Single women knew of the hardships involved in a pioneering existence and preferred to seek employment in towns as maids or in the service industry. In 1911, 53 per cent of Finnish women in Port Arthur were working as domestics or as hotel staff.[16] Running a farm, even a primitive subsistence homestead, however, required co-operation between men and women. Some bachelors did try homesteading alone but soon realized that their future success depended on their ability to find a strong, hard-working woman to share the load. The best prospects were women who had just arrived from the old country and were not yet spoiled by Canadian ways. Taimi's mother, Kirsti Loviisa Korhonen, sailed to Canada in the spring of 1910 and travelled directly to her brother's homestead, a small clearance with a primitive shack, in Kivikoski. She cried and declared that she had never been so disappointed in her life and she bitterly regretted her decision to move to Canada. She made immediate plans to seek employment in Port Arthur and to save enough money for a return ticket to Finland. Her brother, David, realized that the only way to keep Kirsti in Kivikoski was to introduce her at once to one of the local bachelors. He hastily arranged a meeting with Antti Pitkänen, a Finn who had immigrated to Canada three years earlier. The clandestine plan worked; in July of 1910, just months after the young couple met, they were married.

For the next 22 years, they endured a life of endless work, sleep deprivation, ill health, poverty, and isolation. The pragmatic young couple started their life in a "lean-to," a one-room shack with a slanted roof. For wedding presents, they bought each other a sack of flour, and someone gave the young couple a calf. The next year, Kirsti cleared land, started a vegetable garden, tried to construct a small cabin better suited for human habitation, and endured a mosquito-filled summer and a bitterly cold winter. Much of this time, she was entirely alone. In order to survive, her husband had to seek work with the Grand Trunk Railway and hunt and fish for food. For seven months of the first year, she was also pregnant with twins. The delivery of the babies, who were born prematurely on 3 August 1911, was long and potentially fatal for Taimi. No medical assistance was available, although two neighbouring women came to help with the birth. One twin, Taimi, was a healthy infant, but her sister, Taru, was disabled and partially paralyzed for life. Kirsti had no time to recuperate. Animals, farm work, and now two infants, one of them severely disabled, demanded her constant attention. Soon, Kirsti was pregnant again, and, on 30 January 1913, a brother, Aate Veli, was born. To say that life for this pioneer immigrant woman was hard is an understatement.

Taimi, an observant child, sympathized with her mother and other women like her in the neighbouring homesteads. Taimi remembered: "Three of us born in a year and a half and my sister a cripple and still they lived in the bush with nothing. Mother had physical health problems left from her child-births which were never corrected. She had to get out of her child-birth bed immediately, lifting heavy pails, etc.— not getting any time to heal or rest. There were no doctors, no money and they lived too far in the bush to get help. Poor people didn't go to the doctor until they were near death or until it was too late. There were no check-ups, no medicine, no relief from drudgery and shortage of many basic foods, especially during the non-growing months."

To protect her children from injury and accidents, make them into productive contributors to the family's survival, and, perhaps, take out the frustrations and anger of her own hard life, Kirsti demanded strict obedience from her children at all times. Taimi explained: "We could never oppose or even show disapproval at home [*Ei saanut olla suu väärässä*] and you couldn't ask any questions. Mother beat that out of us. I lived to please my mother, I was just terrified of her. She was very hard, very abusive. There was no embracing in my family, none, not ever. Consequently I did not know how to comfort her either, and silently I cried." Both Taimi and Aate excelled in school, winning awards and advancing quickly. Taru could not attend school as her partial paralysis made it impossible for her to travel the distance from home. Taimi's home encouraged reading, especially reading politically relevant material, yet she was ultimately denied the opportunity for higher education. She recalled: "Mother allowed us to read but not too much. She did not want us to become '*kirjatoukkas*' [bookworms] and be absent-minded. She said that workers had to be always working and they couldn't be day-dreaming about nonsensical books. We were encouraged to read the newspapers which mother subscribed to and our school books. After graduation there was no money to send two of us to secondary school in Port Arthur so I stayed home and my only brother went to Port Arthur Tech and passed with honours."

Injustices caused by poverty, poor health care, and the unequal treatment of women had left Kirsti bitter and thoroughly frustrated. One event, in particular, enraged both Kirsti and Taimi and left them distrustful of the capitalist society and the bureaucracy that served it. From the time they were toddlers, Taimi had cared for her twin sister. Since Taru never left the homestead, she spoke only Finnish. Her mind was fine, but her education was simply neglected. When Taru was 12 years old, the authorities took her from her home to "go to school." Her parents approved and captured the happy departure in a photograph in which Taru, clinging to her doll and nestled next to her dog, was smiling. Rather than to school, however, Taru was taken to a Fort William hospital, and from there she was sent to another hospital "for the incurables" in Orillia, Ontario. For months, the young child was kept in full body cast. She was unable to communicate or to see her family; the Pitkänen's had no money for Kirsti to travel to Orillia.

Taimi worried about her sister and cried whenever she thought of her amongst strangers, unable to speak English, and not understanding

why no one came to visit her. She also sympathized with the silent suffering of her mother. Then came the news that Taru was dying. Some-
how, with the help of neighbours, Kirsti managed to scrape enough
money together to take the train to Orillia and reached the bedside of
her daughter just two days before she died in August 1926. She found
Taru in deplorable condition, neglected and full of festering bedsores.
Kirsti, remembering her happy-go-lucky child, concluded that the authorities had, in less than three years, killed Taru. Kirsti blamed herself and regretted her inability to have any impact on her child's life.
She resented being treated as an inconsequential nuisance, but, unable
to speak English, she felt utterly helpless. She cried, but no one com-
forted her, and her frustration and bitterness grew into anger. Kirsti's
resolve to change the capitalist system was cemented with the tragic
death of her daughter. Taru's death also changed Taimi's life forever.
She had loved her sister dearly and never forgot the hard lesson she
learnt from her death: the authorities were not to be trusted. They did
not care about the poor or immigrants. Taru's death also made Taimi
the vehicle of her mother's ambition to change the capitalist system.

FARM WOMEN'S ORGANIZED ACTIVITY
Mercifully, the lives of the women of Kivikoski held more than
work and tragedy. Women sought solace from each other and their
community; although physically cut off from the rest of the world,
their spirits and imagination soared far beyond the Kivikoski boundaries. The women were literate in Finnish, and many spent their free
time reading whatever Finnish-language material they could find.
Typically, they read left-wing newspapers, especially the *Toveritar*
(Female Comrade), a socialist Finnish women's newspaper printed in
Astoria, Oregon, between 1911 and 1930. The library was also in good
use.

The Kivikoski Finns, like many other Finnish immigrants before
1930, had acquired socialist beliefs in their homeland. The Social Democratic Party (SDP) had exploded into existence and become the
largest political party in Finland around the time of Antti and Kirsti

Pitkänen's emigration. The SDP of Finland fought for women's emancipation, legal, and political rights. In 1906, Finnish women became
the first women in any country to obtain full political rights, and, in
1907, 19 women were elected as members of Finland's first unicam-
eral parliament. One of the nine women Members of Parliament who
represented the SDP 1907–1909 moved to the United States in 1910
and, a year later, became the founding editor of *Toveritar*. Through its
pages, Maria Raunio tried to bridge the gap between socialist women
in Finland and Finnish women in North America. Although she only
published eight issues before committing suicide, subsequent editors
of *Toveritar* continued to include information on both the North
American and Finnish socialist women's movements.[17]

The upsurge of socialism in Finland met strong opposition. Many
socialist leaders were forced to flee Finland during the repressive reign
of Czar Nicholas II who tried to restrict the autonomy of his Grand
Duchy, Finland, which had been established in 1809. After Finland
gained independence from Russia in 1917, a bitter civil war took place
between the socialist "Red" Finns and the government's "White"
forces. In three bloody months of battle, 80,000 Finns died - some perished in battle; others were starved in concentration camps or executed
by the victorious White Guard. The post-civil war era witnessed an
unprecedented exodus of Finns to Canada. Many of the new arrivals
had supported the "Red" forces. Included among this group of immigrants were some of the movement's capable leaders and the socialist
prime minister of Finland, Oskari Tokoi. Finnish immigrants soon discovered that the lot of workers in Canada was not much better than in
their homeland. Indeed, in many instances, the injustices they faced as
marginalized immigrants were even worse than their life in Finland.

To improve their lives and working conditions, Finns in Canada
founded socialist groups that espoused modest versions of familiar socialist societies in their homeland. In 1911, the scattered groups of
Finnish socialists joined an umbrella organization called the Finnish
Socialist Organization of Canada (FSOC), a group that would later
simply be known as the Finnish Organization of Canada (FOC). In the

fall of 1911, within a year of Kirsti and Antti Pitkänen's marriage, Kivikoski Finns joined the FSOC under the Port Arthur Charter.[18] By 1914, 39 of Kivikoski's approximately 60 residents had joined the FSOC, which had grown to be a powerful national organization consisting of 64 locals across Canada and 3,062 members. It remained the largest and most influential Finnish organization in Canada until the Second World War.

At first, some Finnish socialist groups also affiliated with the Socialist Party of Canada (SPC). Port Arthur Finns joined the SPC in 1907, forming the Port Arthur Finnish Socialist Local #6. In 1911, complaining that the SPC was too restrictive and "dogmatic," they, along with the entire FSOC became a staunch supporter of the newly founded Worker's Party, later called the Communist Party of Canada (CPC). In 1925, the CPC reported 4,500 members of whom 3,100 were Finnish - perhaps 30 to 40 per cent of these individuals were woman. The Finnish community encouraged, even expected, its women to lend their support to the FSOC. The FOC, and the Canadian political parties with which it was affiliated.[19]

Kirsti Pitkänen did not need any coaxing to join the FSOC. She was a determined woman. The frustration, anger, and defiance she felt could take many forms, some of them destructive, others constructive. Although living in isolation and extreme poverty. "She was so ahead of her times," said Taimi. With her limited means, she fought for women's rights and political suffrage and insisted on keeping her own small earnings. Taimi explained: "Mother was the first woman in her neighbourhood to cut her hair short—oh my—that was a brave thing to do. She kept a jar where she put the little money she earned from selling butter. 'My money is not going to any man's back pocket,' she used to say. The luxuries she ordered with her money included the *Toveritar* newspaper which was her real friend and which she read from cover to cover. She started to go to meetings with other local farm women. They were a tough bunch; men nicknamed them "ton-and-a-half-women.'"

At first, the women met in small groups in each other's homes; even after the school and the hall were built, they preferred the less intimidating and more social setting of private homes. At these small gatherings, women discussed their private problems and concerns. Often, they brought knitting or sewing along. They shared farming tips, worries about their children, and ideas about health, education, and family planning. Many later commented that much of the discussion centred on men and their lack of understanding of women's work and hardships. Through their community effort and food donations, women made sure that the Kivikoski school was able to offer students free hot lunches, a good library, and the opportunity to play musical instruments and sports. They staged an annual fair in which competitions were held between the Kivikoski school and schools from other Finnish communities in public speaking, sports, music, and academic subjects. In 1927, the more than 40 students of the one-room Kivikoski school were dissatisfied with their teacher and, with the support of the community, had enough confidence to stage a successful strike.[20]

Increasingly, the Kivikoski women also focused on their own needs and utilized their meetings for self-improvement and educational purposes. They encouraged each other to enhance their public speaking skills, read socialist literature, and write to socialist newspapers. Discussions became more structured and followed some prearranged theme designed to increase women's class-consciousness. As the confidence of the women rose, their activities became more ambitious, their goals more far-reaching, and their contribution to the FOC more significant. Still women usually held only supportive roles within the FOC. They organized bazaars, cooked the meals at picnics and dances, fed striking lumber workers in Port Arthur, and signed petitions.

Women were also active supporters of the co-operative movement. They could sell their extra milk, butter, and eggs to the Finnish-run Thunder Bay Co-operative Dairy and the International Co-operative Stores in exchange for consumer products. While men held most of the leadership positions in the co-operatives (Taimi's father, for example, served on the executive of one) women's active support was crucial to their success.

In 1921, the Kivikoski Finns built themselves a new meeting place, a proper hall with a stage, a library, and good kitchen facilities.[21] Kirsti became one of the hall' most dedicated volunteers. She had more time to devote to political organization and other causes as her children were growing older. The CPC, which had set up a Woman's Department in 1924 and appointed Florence Constance its first director. encouraged all existing women's groups to join the Women's Labour League (WLL). The FOC facilitated a smooth transition of the Finnish women's auxiliaries into the WLL locals—according to Finnish sources, the locals became 95 per cent Finnish.[22]

The Kivikoski women's group officially affiliated with the WLL on 27 June 1927. In reality, its activity did not change a great deal. As all members were Finnish-speaking, they continued to meet, as usual, in private homes. Attendance was uneven, especially when the members' children were small or when the weather rendered the road impassable. The founding members described themselves as "old women," although many had not yet reached the age of 40. Those who were able to attend the meeting found that the gathering provided a brief, but important, respite from work. For most, the social interaction was more important than the political goals. "When the day of the meeting arrives," reported one Kivikoski woman in *Toveritar*, "one is able to leave home for a little while, and announce to the family member staying behind that 'I am going to a meeting.' Going to meetings is fun, as we take turns visiting each other's homes." As members of the WLL, Kivikoski women seemed to gain more independence, and women were able to make important new alliances beyond the FOC. The evolving sisterhood also manifested itself in its demand for more travelling female speakers who would focus specifically on farm women's issues.[23]

WLL members in Kivikoski decided to subscribe to the communist newspaper *The Woman Worker*. Most Finnish women could not read the English-language paper, but they wanted to support the larger cause it represented and hoped that their daughters would benefit from it. They were extremely proud that a Finnish woman had designed the cover of *The Woman Worker*. Moreover, the cover depicted two goals close to their hearts—"a woman holding a book, symbolizing Knowledge, and a flame, representing Enlightenment." Nonetheless, the Finnish women were quite puzzled, and even disappointed, with the *Woman Worker*. They were particularly concerned that it was published so infrequently (monthly) and was so modest in size and appearance. Their own Finnish-language newspaper, *Toveritar*, published in Astoria, Oregon, was supported by subscriptions and the radical left-wing Finnish organizations in North America. It was regular multi-page weekly newspaper with over 12,000 subscribers, of whom 3,000 lived in Canada. The newspaper also had an "army of correspondents" from at least 122 communities across Canada.[24] Although *Toveritar* offered serious political articles, the women of Kivikoski "enjoyed most the serialized fictional stories." Kirsti Pitkänen was in charge of subscriptions in her community, and the women from Kivikoski submitted reports of their activities to the *Toveritar*. In addition, women also read *Vapaus*, a newspaper published in Sudbury, Ontario, which had very close links with the FOC. Taimi's father was responsible for obtaining subscriptions to *Vapaus* in Kivikoski.

One of the questions frequently raised in the WLL meetings and openly debated within the FOC was the role of farm women in left-wing politics and in the Communist Party of Canada. Why should they be organized? How could they demand a minimum wage, a shorter workday, and longer holidays? Who would give them maternity leave or accident benefits? Were they to strike against their husbands, children or farm animals? How could the party make farm women, especially subsistence farm women, aware of their class position? *Toveritar*, which echoed the views of the Workers Party of America, the Communist Party of Canada, and the left-wing immigrants in North America, admitted that farm women's concerns had not been adequately addressed. In 1927, the paper began to publish a regular section called *"Maalaisnaiset ja perheenemännät"* (rural women and housewives). In this section, women voiced common concerns and wrote about living like "hermits" in total isolation with 18-hour workdays. They also complained that their husbands, their communities, and the organized workers, including other women, did not respect their work. Many of the articles repeated the theme of lack of respect and the violation of human dignity. For example, a woman from Finland, Ontario, sent in comments from her WLL meeting: "We discussed how we could erase barriers between women who live in cities and farm women and how we could work as equals for workers' common cause. Even if it seems to the women who work in industries that women who live on the farm are lagging behind, are backward, as they are in style, they could still treat her as a comrade in struggle... solidarity strengthens the movement, not looking down your noses at farm women,"Farm women supported the WLL out of solidarity with other women out of concern for their children's welfare. In answer to a question, "What is the purpose of the WLL?" a Port Arthur woman replied in *Toveritar*: "Its purpose is to raise and develop us into more informative mothers and educators of our children, so that we can bring up a class-conscious new generation."[25] Sisterhood was another important aspect of the WLL in that the organization provided a network for interaction with other like-minded women. International Women's Day became a celebration that tied the remote farm women to working women around the world. The women of Kivikoski, for example, celebrated with an evening full of entertainment. Some of the most enthusiastic and talented women went to district conventions where they had an opportunity to meet other women organizers and discuss the WLL platform.

EDUCATION OF YOUNG RADICALS

Canada's Finnish immigrant women had always been concerned about the health and welfare of their children. With the advent of the WLL, their focus shifted increasingly to serious political educational work with children and youth. They organized socialist Sunday school meetings and educational summer camps. They encouraged Kivikoski children to join CPC's Young Communist League (YCL) and Young Pioneers. Unlike the adult activities available in the Finnish communities, the young people's programs were conducted in English. The Kivikoski group reported in 1925: "We have already succeeded to a point where all correspondence between the various FOC youth leagues and the district headquarters are in English... we are also asking our youth groups to subscribe and distribute the newspaper *Young Worker*."[26]

Given that immigrant students were constantly the subject of "Canadianization" efforts—attempts to assimilate them into Anglo-Canadian customs and ideals—in schools, women realized that they faced a tough fight to pass on their socialist ideals to their children. The parents lamented that most Canadians were hostile towards progressive ideas and labour struggles. To counteract the "propaganda" from schools, they had to organize and win the young minds of their off-spring. The FOC advised parents that the most important component in educating class-conscious children was to set a good example at home. If mothers went to meetings and were active, daughters would follow. Better yet, women ought to bring their older daughters to the meetings with them. Furthermore, it was important to give young people inter-esting activities that could entice them to bond together. Sports, arts, and educational classes should be intermixed with political instruction. The goal was to fight against the religious instruction and imperialist sentiment taught in the school system. In 1928, the WLL's Northern Ontario District meeting demanded that schools ban religious instruc-tion, stop inciting children to war, and forbid corporeal punishment. In addition, it demanded school boards give free hot meals and books to all students and, as necessary, clothing to needy students. Finally, it encouraged parents to do everything in their power to send young peo-ple to camps and youth leadership courses so that they could become the backbone of the future labour movement. Kivikoski residents or-ganized youth leagues that conformed to the expectations of the YCL. An account from Kivikoski in March 1929 reported considerable activ-ity despite severe winter conditions, "Eleven members of the youth or-ganization meet regularly every other Sunday... The young people or-ganized an entertainment evening on the 23 of March where a two-act play *'Mieron tiellä' [Life of a Beggar]* was performed... The young people also have gymnastics classes every Sunday directed by Matti Hoxell. We have already had one agitation meeting and hope to organ-ize more as soon as we have new themes. The *'Seinälehti'* [hand-written newspaper written by the members, which hangs from the wall of the hall for all to read] has been published..."[27]

At the time of the report, approximately 18 teenagers lived in the community. Considering the difficulties many of them faced in regard to travel and illness, the participation rate was very high. The report ended by describing the funeral of one of the young female members, Aili Kainulainen, who had died after a lengthy illness. Aili was

Taimi's nearest neighbour in Kivikoski. Her mother had died of tuberculosis in 1922, leaving five children, three of whom also slowly succumbed the the same disease.[28] The family had no money for doctors and no relief from farm chores. The family briefly hired a Finnish immigrant woman to help with the children, but she could not endure the hardships and committed suicide by drinking lye. The heavy responsibility of raising children now fell on the oldest living daughter, 14-year-old Ellen. Taimi recalls that "Ellen never had time to visit or come to the hall. She could not participate in the YCL. She was always doing chores."

Tragedy was common and life a constant struggle in the community. The children were not only the objects of their parents' ambitions, but also bore the brunt of their anger, frustrations, alcoholism, and insanity. If medical help for physical illness was difficult to find, emotional and mental problems went completely without treatment. One Kivikoski family, notorious for their child abuse, did not allow their children to interact at all with other children. Two of these children committed suicide to escape the violence, and one of the daughters became a Port Arthur prostitute. In another family, 15-year-old Impi Virtanen shot herself at home in Kivikoski "after fighting with her widowed mother." The other alternative available to desperate teenagers with abusive parents was to fight back. Thus, Taimi's school friend Veikko Lyytinen, at the age of 15, dug himself into a snowbank, waited for his father to come home, and then shot him. The father is described in *Vapaus* as having been 'inhumanely cruel towards his family." The Kivikoski community rallied in the son's defence, but he received a two-year jail sentence for his crime. The newspaper reported that he was "much happier in jail than at home."[29] The exceptionally harsh reality of these teenagers' experience reportedly served to their more fortunate schoolmates as a reminder of capitalism's downside.

The abject poverty of the subsistence farmers and their constant toil with few rewards strengthened the Kivikoski teenagers' resolve to support socialist solutions. Taimi's parents, although strict disciplinarians and not alien to harsh punishment, encouraged active participation and socializing with other youths in the community. The Pitkänen farm, nicknamed *"Käpälämäki"* (place to run away to), had beautiful rolling hills where youngsters gathered for cross-country skiing and tobogganing. During the summer, the children occasionally had picnics, berry-picking excursions, and fishing trips in nearby Hazelwood Lake on the Pitkänens' small boat, *Lenin*. Frequent family saunas, which were an essential part of every Finnish home, offered an invigorating break, especially when combined with the cultural tradition of rolling naked in the snow.

Except for epidemics and accidents, the Kivikoski children's general health was quite good. Public health nurses who inspected rural children in the Thunder Bay and Rainy River districts during the summer of 1925 concluded: "the majority of the Finnish children seen are healthy and well nourished." One nurse attributed their good health to their lifestyle: "The Finnish people live very simply and plainly as to diet; their homes are clean and airy and even the poorest of them have a bath house (sauna) which is used almost daily." Another commented that "even in the most remote corners one finds the Finn with cows and garden." The nurses were pleased to observe that Finnish school children did not suffer from head lice and had clean fingernails.[30] Striving for physical fitness and cleanliness was part of the Finnish cultural ideals that Kivikoski Finns had brought to Canada. Photographs of Kivikoski Young Pioneers or school children display healthy looking youngsters. Taimi commented, "There were no fat children, obesity was unheard of. We worked so hard with our chores, we were outdoors in the fresh air most of the time, and we certainly did not get any sweet foods."

Taimi and her brother Aate were two of the most active Young Pioneers in Kivikoski. The radicalization of young Taimi and Aate began at home and was reinforced by the community. Their mother, realizing that her language difficulties and poor health would never allow her to make a major political contribution in Canada beyond her Finnish ethnic community, began to prepare her son and daughter for this greater political activism. Taimi explained, "Mother took us to the Finnish hall but she did not allow us to come unless we had some performance rehearsed. We had to practise all week to recite a poem, give a speech, play our instruments, sing or tell a story, or act something. I was terrified, I was so nervous, but it didn't matter. Mother wanted us to learn to speak in public, she wanted us to have a voice and to have opinions and we didn't dare to go against her will."

Taimi became an "eager beaver" within the socialist movement. She carried her mother's hopes on her shoulders, and her mother expected her to become a great socialist speaker, agitator, and leader. The education of the young radical that had begun with the public performances at the hall continued in YCL camps held in various locations around Thunder Bay. At these camps, the children learned politics and economics from the workers' perspective. Great Canadian socialist teachers and leaders such as A.E. Smith, a person who left a lasting impression on Taimi, inspired them. Finnish agitators, who criss-crossed the North American Finnish communities, also trained them. Martin Hendrickson from the United States and Sanna Kannasto from rural Thunder Bay most impressed Taimi.

Kannasto became a role model for Taimi and other socialist Finish women in Canada. She made her first cross-Canada tour as a paid Finnish socialist agitator in 1907. Her task was to pull all the isolated socialist groups into one great organization. Kannasto was a tremendous speaker and an extraordinary organizer who paid special attention to organizing women. Her arrests and imprisonment in both the United States and Canada had made her a legendary figure. She was respected even among her neighbours despite the fact that her forcefulness and critical comments often offended them.[31] Taimi's mother wanted her daughter to become like Sanna Kannasto and, perhaps, to be her successor. When Taimi was a young teenager, her mother sent her to live with Kannasto in her small subsistence farm in the nearby Finnish rural community of North Branch. "My mother thought that I should learn from Sanna Kannasto. She thought that Sanna could teach me public speaking and revolutionary ideas. Sanna was a revolutionary, a very strong feminist and always well-informed, which I was not. I spent ten days with her because my mother thought it would be a good idea. I was just a farm girl, a peasant, it was hard to understand her."

In 1925, at the age of 14, Taimi began to attend meetings and became a full member of the Kivikoski women's group. Taimi has fond memories of her early political activism: "In every meeting we discussed politics, women, and workers. We made '*ponsilauseita*' (resolutions) and sent appeals and petitions to the government. We worked with the Labour Defence League (LDL) to which we also belonged. We held socials, auctioned baskets, had *kalakukko* ['fish-rooster', a special Finnish bread filled with fish] festivities and my mother was the *kalakukko* master. We had *ukot ja tytöt* [men and girls] versus *akat ja pojat* [women and boys] teams which competed against each other and always we had *pulla* [sweet bread] and coffee."

In 1928, when Taimi was 18, the Kivikoski women chose her, along with her mother, to be a delegate at the Port Arthur District WLL convention held in Fort William. The meeting, chaired by Sanna Kannasto, had representatives from 10 WLL Port Arthur District locals, including 6 from the small rural communities surrounding Port Arthur. The majority of the delegates represented farm women. Unlike some other WLL Districts in southern Ontario and Western Canada where the membership consisted of women from many ethnic groups, all of the Port Arthur District No. 6 delegates were Finnish women.

Many of the convention's agenda items dealt with youth involvement; indeed, the convention decided to hold instructional summer camps for young people. Sanna Kannasto agreed to continue tutoring promising youngsters in public speaking at her home, and the delegates decided to establish a special rotating library for the Young Pioneers. They also proposed that special efforts be made to protect the young people from the perils of alcohol, which, the women agreed, was an evil curse in their communities. Other items of the agenda included decisions to support the LDL and the co-operative movement, which was seen as an important safeguard against the capitalist forces for subsistence farmers. Women were also eager to have civil marriages legalized. Their strong anti-clerical sentiments prevented many from getting married by a minister of the church. Common-law marriages, recognized by the Finnish community but not by the authorities, left women vulnerable and unable to collect compensation if their husbands died in industrial accidents.[32]

At a WLL convention held the following year, the women concluded that the Port Arthur District's greatest challenge was to try to entice English-speaking women and women from other ethnic groups to join the organization. They hoped that the second generation would be more successful in integrating with non-Finnish women and bringing them into the meetings.[33] However, in 1930, when the CPC decided to integrate all workers' activity into one workers' Unity League, Finnish women continued to meet in each others' homes. Although the support of the CPC for independent women's organizations had provided more structure and common themes for women to discuss, the cultural bonds, common language, and need for social interaction among "like-minded women" guaranteed the continuance of separate women's organized activity in Kivikoski.

STUDY IN THE SOVIET UNION

The Great Depression hit most immigrant communities in Canada very hard. Self-sufficient in food and fuel, Kivikoski fared better than urban Finntowns and was even able to ship food to hungry unemployed workers and striking lumber workers in Port Arthur. Still, an air of pessimism and hopelessness pervaded the community. Young men experienced few work opportunities outside the community, and their future looked bleak. Upon graduation from the Kivikoski school, some drifted to the cities only to join the army of unemployed. The increasing harassment of immigrant radicals by the authorities and conflicts within the Finnish left-wing community itself made the situation worse. Royal Canadian Mounted Police and government intimidation tactics included sudden house searches, seizures of literature, arrests, and deportations. The community was especially incensed over the imprisonment of Arvo Vaara, editor of *Vapaus*. In February 1929,

Vaara was sentenced to serve six months in Burwash Industrial Farm for showing disrespect to King George V. Vaara had suggested that the health of the King did not matter in comparison to the curse of the capitalist system.[34] A month later, police charged eight members of the FOC with breaking the *Lord's Day Act* by organizing or attending a concert on Sunday. Two years later, Vaara and Martin Parker, assistant editor of *Vapaus*, were arrested again and deported. In November 1929, soon after the stock market crash helped precipitate the Great Depression, Canada banned *Toveritar* and some other left-wing Finnish language newspapers published in the United States. This measure deprived Finnish-Canadian radical women of their means of communication and their public voice.[35]

While the left-wing Finns had dominated Finnish-Canadian organized life, they were splintered and unable to form a strong "united front". Unlike Kivikoski, which was rather uniform in its support of the FOC and the Communist Party of Canada, other Finnish communities, especially in Sault Ste Marie and Port Arthur, associated also with the Industrial Workers of the World (IWW), which was organizing lumber workers. After a major internal dispute in 1932, the more social democratic Finns within the FOC formed their own organizations, which initially supported the CCF. New, conservative groups of Finns that organized during the late 1920s as the Loyal Finns of Canada, also hindered the growth of the Finnish left. These groups allied with the Lutheran Church and were even harsher critics of the Finnish radicals than the Canadian government. The antagonism was clearly demonstrated when bush workers went on strike.

In the Thunder Bay region, strikes not only revealed the disunity of the Finnish-Canadian left but also pitted union organizers against Finnish subcontractors working in the area.[36] In 1929, two union representatives of the Lumber Workers Industrial Union, Viljo Rosvall and John Voutilainen, disappeared during an organizing trip to the Pigeon River Lumber Company at Onion Lake, 30 kilometers from Port Arthur. Finnish communities around Port Arthur patrolled the woods all winter searching for the two men or their murderers and, in the spring, found the bodies of the two organizers in a shallow creek. Taimi's brother Aate made the grizzly discovery of one of the bodies. While the official verdict was that the men had drowned, the community was convinced that Finnish lumber camp owners opposed to unions had murdered the experienced woodsmen. On 28 April 1930, thousands of people (2,000 according to the *News Chronicle*, 5,000 according to union sources) "joined in the largest funeral cortege that ever passed through the streets of Port Arthur."[37] To the Finns, the official investigation of the death of Rosvall and Voutilainen was a sham and just another example of the injustice foreign workers had to endure in Canada. Taimi recalled, "Voutilainen was well known to all of us. He owned a homestead in the community of Tarmola near us. We all went to the funeral. I remember that there was an eclipse which really left an eerie feeling to the whole demonstration. There were thousands of people. It was such a shame, we were all sure that the men were murdered."

Against this background of depression, harassment, anti-union sentiment, and disunity among the Finnish Canadians, the Soviet Union seemed like the new land of promise and opportunity for many of the most radical Finnish immigrants. During the late 1920s and early 1930s, CPC policies were increasingly dictated from the Soviet Union, which encouraged educational tours to Moscow for the party's Canadian leaders. Some Canadian political organizers went to the Soviet Union for extensive periods to study communism in action and to observe the success of the Soviet Union's planned economy. In 1930, Becky Buhay of the CPC's Women's Department, decided to lead a women's delegation to the U.S.S.R. After protests that Finnish women had been excluded from a project that Finnish members of the WLL had largely funded, Elsa Tynjälä, a domestic from northern Ontario, was permitted to join the "women's tour." Tynjälä proved to be a disappointment to the CPC as she, upon her return, did not feel comfortable speaking in English in public. She did, however, write a few travel accounts in Finnish that were published in *Vapaus*.[38]

While the women's tour was a public propaganda event, other Canadians travelled to the Soviet Union unnoticed and in secret. These included youth leaders from the YCL. Taimi had been singled out as a dedicated member of the YCL and was a logical candidate for such a trip. In 1930, her parents, together with the FOC and the CPC, sent her and four other teenagers to the Soviet Union for intensive training. Arvo Vaara, recently released from prison, organized the year-long visit. "They were looking for young people who would become future leaders and agitators in Canada. The FOC was really pushing this learning and studying." The "timid and scared farm-girl," as Taimi described herself, began making her preparations. "Everything was very secretive. We would live and travel incognito. I became Liz Alton. I made the name up really quickly and then I forgot my new name." She could not say goodbye to friends, and Taimi was asked not to contact anyone in Canada after her arrival in the Soviet Union. Three young boys and a girl accompanied her on the trip, one boy from the Port Arthur area, two from the Sudbury area, and a 15-year-old girl, Kyllikki (Irma) Mantere, from the neighbouring rural community of North Branch. Kyllikki chose the name of Anne Walters, a name she kept for the rest of her life. Because Anne was under-aged, the organizers asked Taimi to act as her guardian. All five students in the group leaving for the Soviet Union were, in fact, teenage children of Finnish immigrants.

Life for the young revolutionaries in the Soviet Union was difficult indeed. Two of the young boys were shipped back upon arrival in Leningrad for their drunken behaviour during the trip. "Liz" and "Anne" were deemed to be too young and lacking in trade union experience to attend the Western Minorities University in Leningrad. Instead they were sent to Moscow to attend the international Young communist League School, where they lived in dormitories and studied with other prospective communist youth leaders from all around the world. "Quite a few were from the United States and Australia but there were others too, such as Germans and Chinese. We studied in English but we heard quite a bit of Finnish too." Many lifelong friendships were

cemented amongst this hand-picked group of future communist leaders. Taimi recalled, "I left my heart in Moscow, I really did. He was a
German, also a student like us. I doubt he ever survived the purges in
Germany, as the Nazis got rid of all the labour radicals during the Second World War." The students toured the Soviet Union in order to see
the five-year plan in action. Taimi was the only girl to travel north, all
the way to Archangel, where she did "political work," which meant
"practical work." She visited farming communes and factories and
learned how the Soviet system worked. In Moscow, she studied Marxism, Leninism, and other political theories. "We studied all the 'isms':
fascism, imperialism, capitalism, socialism, communism. It was hard,
too hard; we worked and studied all the time. I felt that there were so
many expectations on us when we returned. I felt the stress terribly
and both Anne and I got sick. Anne was so sick that she had to stay in
Moscow an extra year. I had scarlet fever and pleurisy. There was just
so much pressure when you are trying to study and make sense and to
be among people who knew so much. Who was I to be there? I was
from a farm dung-heap up north—what did I know except hard work?
It was a mistake to send us, too much enthusiasm, too many hopes
pinned on us."All Taimi's classmates at the Lenin School in Moscow
were young adults enrolled in the Communist "Party Course." Many
Canadian labour leaders, such as Sam Scarr, Harvey Murphy, and
Stewart Smith, had taken the two-year course. Among the adults
studying to be better agitators and labour leaders, according to Taimi,
were also many Canadians from the Finnish, Ukrainian, and Jewish
communities. Taimi regrets not remembering their names: "it wasn't
expedient to know, there was a lot of secrecy about everything." The
secrecy extended to Taimi's return trip in August of 1931. Before her
return to Canada, she learned well-rehearsed stories of travel abroad
that she was to recount to conceal her activities in the Soviet Union.

Quite separate from the planned educational tours organized for
radical leaders and students was a mass migration of dissatisfied Finnish immigrants to the Soviet Union. Between 1930 and 1935, several
thousand Finnish Canadians caught the "Karelia fever" and decided to

relocate in Soviet Karelia, a district just east of the Finnish border. This region was rich in mythic Finnish connotations and possessed a beautiful, rugged terrain and many Finnish-speaking residents. This voluntary exodus began with enthusiasm and amid fervent hopes of building a new "socialist utopia" in Soviet Karelia.[39] About a third of those who left eventually returned to Canada, but the fate of the others was dismal. Most able-bodied adult men fell victim to the Stalinist purges of 1937–1938. They were executed, starved to death in forced labour camps, or exiled to Siberia. Josef Stalin, leader of the Soviet Union, was purging his country of suspected "enemies of the state." Women and children suffered horribly as well, and many were exiled to Siberia.

In Canada, the FOC organized this mass movement of Finns, and many of the people who left were the organization's most enthusiastic members. Thus, capable Finnish WLL leaders such as Mary North, Anna Apponen, and Martta Lehto, moved to Soviet Karelia. All lost their husbands to the purges, and the first two women died of starvation and disease. Martta Lehto Survived to tell her story. A 1988 interview with her in the city of Petrozavodsk in Eastern Karelia revealed the atrocities in their full horror. Martta Lehto, who had been a teacher in YCL summer camps and a founding member of the Blairmore, Alberta, WLL, was especially distraught over the fate of her students who fell victim to the purges. One example of former YCL members victimized in Soviet Karelia is a group of boys from Port Arthur. As they had been accustomed to doing in Canada, they had organized a band, or "*penikkabändi*" (puppy band), and rehearsed in Petrozavodsk on Sundays. One sunday morning, all the teenage boys were "taken" never to be seen again. Recent investigations indicate that most likely they were all shot.

The "Karelia fever" also spread to Kivikoski. Many of its residents sold everything they owned, and some borrowed money from family and neighbours, in order to travel to Soviet Karelia. The young people of Kivikoski had accepted their parents' positive views of the Soviet Union. Their futures also seemed bleak in Canada. Fearing unemployment and looking forward to building a socialist state, recently graduated young men, all members of the Kivikoski YCL, departed from the Port Arthur railway station in a party atmosphere. Among the first to leave was Taimi's brother Aate, who died in the Soviet Union during the Second World War. Other Kivikoski-born boys, all sons of WLL activists, who departed in 1931 included Matti Hoxell and Tauno Peterson. The niece of the first Kivikoski teacher, Martha Rissanen, also left. Upon release from prison, young Veikko Lyytinen, the teenager who had shot his father, decided to leave Kivikoski forever and seek a new life in Soviet Karelia. Taimi's two uncles, Martti and Aatu Pitkänen, and their wives were among the farmers who left. Taimi's father resisted the temptation for four years, but then he too left for Karelia in 1935. His wife, suffering from ill health, refused to leave and was left alone to tend to the farm. Taimi's father returned disillusioned to Kivikoski after two years in the Soviet Union. The parents and brother of Anne Walters, Taimi's travel companion in the U.S.S.R., also moved to Karelia. Kivikoski, with an adult population that barely reached 100, never recovered from the loss of so many of its activists.

CANADIAN LABOUR LEADER AND ORGANIZER

When Taimi returned to Canada, the "red scare" of the Great Depression had focused attention on the unemployed. The deportation of immigrants was on the increase. The Finnish community had a great need for capable organizers, especially since so many had left for Soviet Karelia. Taimi was weary of the expectations that the Communist Party of Canada had placed on her shoulders. She felt inadequate and was worried she would disappoint the Party. She concluded: "I was timid, scared, and not a militant revolutionary. But I was honest and I worked hard. I prided myself on being reliable. In the end I succeeded in political life because I was so conscientious and disciplined." Upon her return to Canada, the YCL sent Taimi to Sudbury to work as a youth organizer. "My job was to educate the youth, to teach them about the conditions of the working class and Marxism. We tried to make them learn the other side of the capitalist society and their place in it. The students were mainly Ukrainians and Finns but there were others too, Canadians and Jews mainly. They were all children of progressive parents, working class children, often from very poor immigrant homes."

In addition, Taimi took part in CPC activities and rallies and served as the secretary of the WLL in Sudbury. The 1930s were a difficult but opportune time for socialist organizers. Unemployed, discouraged men, many of them recent immigrants, filled the streets. These men had the will and the time to protest and march. The biggest labour protests were reserved for the May Day (labour) parades. In May 1932, Taimi was ready to march in Sudbury with her Young Pioneers when riots erupted. The march had hardly begun when spectators noticed that the Union Jack was missing and instead only a red flag fluttered defiantly. The *Sudbury Star* noted, "The emblem of the Soviet Union flapping in the breeze was like a red flag to a bull." This situation was the last straw to many Canadian patriots who had criticized immigrants, especially the Finns in Sudbury, for the lack of respect they had shown to King George V and British rule. Some YCL members had refused to stand up in school assemblies for the singing of "God Save the King." Taimi and her Young Pioneers ended up in the midst of the Sudbury riots. The police singled out Taimi as a dangerous leader, arrested her, and imprisoned her along with 17 other demonstrators, 2 of whom were women. The 4 May issue of the *Sudbury Star* published photographs of those arrested. Taimi was featured in this report: her picture was displayed in the centre of the page and was double the size of those depicting the others arrested with her. The *Sudbury Star* headlines stated bluntly: "18 arrested in battle over Flag as Communists Attempt May Day Parade; Spectators Attack Communists When Union Jack Ignored: Stones, Clubs and Fists fly."

The demonstration turned bloody: "After a pitched battle in which citizens gave liberal assistance to the police, 18 persons were lodged in the cells, most of them with broken heads, and their parade was stopped before it started." Taimi was described as a "Young Pioneers organizer in the communist youth movement, who led the children in organized cheering in the park." The police charged Taimi, now 20 years old, with being a member of an illegal assembly under section 98 of the Criminal Code. According to the *Sudbury Star*, "Four of the men, two Finns and two Ukrainians, arrested in the May Day demonstration were refused bail. Three of them, Mike Kostaniuk, leader in Sunday's demonstration, Kosti Veti and Sam Yurchuk are charged with assaulting a police officer, and Mike Lippenan [sic] is charged with carrying a concealed weapon."

Some men had their bails set at $200, but the three women involved had to come up with $1,000. The sight of dozens of "impertinent little children who had so enthusiastically cried, 'On to the streets'" angered the authorities.[40] Taimi, who in the midst of the Great Depression was penniless, was unable to pay her bail. The FOC eventually raised the money, and she was released after spending two weeks in jail. "When I was arrested I was scared and shocked. The prison doctor gave me a pelvic examination and that was most awkward and embarrassing. I had never had such an examination before. They tried to humiliate me in many ways. We were given soup, bread, and water and that was it for fourteen days. This episode frightened me but it did not stop me, if anything it strengthened my resolve to work for justice."

Imprisonment raised Taimi's profile. She had become the labour movement's latest "victim" and a celebrity among the Sudbury radicals. Soon after her release from prison, she met her future partner and husband, Stephen Forkin, a self-educated scientist and Worker's Unity League organizer. The police arrested Forkin in March of 1932 on charges of sedition, but his case was dismissed. Stewart Smith from the CPC decided to send him from Manitoba, under the name of Jack Davis, to Sudbury to organize unemployed miners and lumber workers in the area.[41]

COMMITMENT FOR LIFE

Taimi Pitkänen (known as Liz Alton in the U.S.S.R.) now took her third name, Mrs. James Davis, and became a dutiful party wife. During the 1930s, she earned some money by cleaning houses in order to support her husband's union organizing activities. They lived in severe poverty, at first in Sudbury and later in Toronto. The couple, in accordance with their anti-clerical custom, lived common-law, announcing their decision to do so in *Vapaus*. On 26 July 1933, they declared, "We Have Joined as Comrades to Each Other." They legalized their marriage years later in Toronto.

Slowly, Taimi grew more distant from FOC activities and the Finnish community, concentrating instead on aiding her husband's political career. Her relationship with her mother, which had been strained from the beginning because it was built on fear and domination, took a nasty turn as Kirsti did not accept her Anglo-Saxon son-in-law. "My mother was disgusted at first," remembers Taimi. She had envisioned a future for her daughter as a militant revolutionary and a feminist leader for the Finnish-Canadian community. But Taimi was content to play a secondary role to her husband. She had always envisioned herself not as a leader but rather as a hard worker for a meaningful cause. She enjoyed supporting some of "the most powerful leftist women like Annie Buller" and her friend and travel companion to the U.S.S.R., Anne Walters, a woman who had "more than lived up to the promise of a dedicated organizer of textile workers." In July of 1933, Anne wrote an enthusiastic letter to her dear friend Taimi. The letter described how 750 striking textile workers—"70% of the strikers were young girls"—had battled the Mercury Mills for three weeks. Another event of note to Anne was the anti-fascist march where the YCL had paraded under their red banner. In 1935, Anne participated in the "on to Ottawa trek right after the riot in Regina." Taimi explained that Anne, "being the capable dedicated and responsible person she always was, was elected to be the leader of the women's contingent."[42]

Taimi's commitment to fight for social justice continued to burn strong, and she worked hard to be supportive of the CPC's causes. "Life," she recalls, "was difficult. We lived in constant fear during the thirties. We never knew who would be knocking on the door." The war years were not much better, except that, for the first time in his life,

Jim Davis was able to get regular work in an aircraft manufacturing plant. As the family's finances improved during the war and as their daughter grew up, Taimi also had more time to devote to her own interests.

She became an active organizer for Women Against Soaring Prices (WASP). In 1959, she joined a group of CPC leaders and made her second trip to the U.S.S.R. in 1960, Taimi Davis, reluctantly agreed to run for public office in Toronto's Ward 8. Her CPC campaign literature reflected the consistency of her life-long goal. In addition to addressing local transportation issues, her platform included proposals for the construction of low rental housing and more schools and hospitals. She was an activist in women's groups opposing nuclear testing and high prices. One of her prized possessions is a certificate from the Canadian Peace Congress in recognition of her work to save Canada and the world from atomic war. Her activities against high food prices continued; in 1973, she was the coordinator of the Etobicoke branch of WASP. The organization, according to Taimi, did not blame farmers for soaring prices. It blamed the corporations and accused them of profiteering. Since 1982, Taimi Davis has been active with the United Senior Citizens of Ontario and has been canvassing support for the indexing of old age pensions. In 1987, she made her third trip to the Soviet Union, a country she admired.[43]

Taimi Davis died in 2005. She lived a life full of purpose, committed to do what she could for social justice. In 1996, the 85-year-old Taimi marched for Mothers against Poverty until she collapsed. In 1997, she announced with enthusiasm, "I just participated in a demonstration at Queen's Park. That was something else, so many people and such enthusiasm. There is a school right next door to this seniors' home and I walk there to support the striking teachers. Some of the seniors here complain that it is noisy because the cars and trucks are honking in support of the teachers but I think it is great, great solidarity."

CONCLUSION

Kivikoski no longer exists as an independent rural community. Its school, hall, and post office have been closed. Nature is reclaiming many of its farms and only a few Finns still inhabit the area. Most of the residents moved away to seek better economic opportunities, but they did not forget their childhood in Kivikoski. During the summer of 1995, the former students of the Kivikoski school (1911–1957) organized a reunion and published a commemorative book that contained 22 articles from different families and photographs of the school days. Not one of the articles, not even the one submitted by Taimi Davis, mentions the Women's Labour League, the Socialist Hall, or the Young Communist League. No hint of Kivikoski's radical past is to be found. The memories are of popular teachers, school fairs and competitions, sports, music, hot meals at school, funny mishaps, and cross-country skiing. Some recall the hardships, poverty, going to school in bare feet, and the frostbites. Except for a few references to classmates who had moved to Karelia, this school reunion publication, although rich in community spirit, entirely hides Kivikoski's political past. Taimi explained, "We live in different times now, it wouldn't be appropriate to write about the politics in such a publication. People are not interested. Things have changed, many people don't want to remember the past. Life was so hard for them during the "red scare" and the cold war. There was the harassment and the stigma, they don't want to make any waves now. Lots of people don't understand, they don't know what life was like for poor immigrant women in the backwoods."

And so the sanitized histories of happy-go-lucky farming communities are born, and the history and legacy of Canada's "ordinary" radical farm women and their children are lost. As a final show of respect for the pioneering farm women of Kivikoski, Taimi Davis agreed to reveal her mother's, and, at the same time, her own, hidden history and all the controversy it contained. Taimi laughed nervously after reading the manuscript: "Oh my, what will people think?" Taimi Davis contributed an important chapter in the history of Canadian women. She described the hardships of Finnish farm women and their gendered division of labour. She also shared their dreams and sorrows, their attempts to build a socialist community, and their efforts to reach out to women beyond Kivikoski. She also documented their attempts to include their children in socialist politics. The radicalization of the Kivikoski children, however, was complex. The poverty and harsh life of the subsistence farmers were not enough to convince the youth to seek alternative solutions to the capitalist system that had dealt them a raw deal. The process involved the example of class-conscious parents, organized radical youth activity, practical training, and a community willing to invest in the political education of its youth. Taimi also revealed how much pain the immigrant parents' impossible expectations caused for their Canadian-born children and how alienating their radical politics were to most Canadians.

The legacy of the radical farm women of northwestern Ontario is also complicated. Radical politics allowed the Kivikoski women to dream beyond their community and to loosen, at least partially, the chains of isolation, both linguistic and geographic, that life in a remote farming community imposed. The children became the mirrors of their mothers' ambition. Their mothers expected them to become both integrated into Canadian radical politics and to stay within the Finnish-Canadian community, which was an impossible choice. They sent Taimi and Anne, for example, to Moscow not realizing that the girls could never return to be leaders of their rural communities or any other Finnish community. Demands for their skills in support of the Canadian radical movement were too strong. Although professing to be international and part of larger working-class movement, ultimately the FOC and the Finnish locals of the WLL served only the first generation Finnish Canadians. The members functioned in Finnish and became protective of their own culture and property. They felt discriminated against and marginalized by the left-wing Canadian political parties into which their children integrated with ease.

Their children, less restricted by language barriers, naturally expanded beyond the Finnish communities. Outside of their farming community, the second generation encountered a wide variety of political and cultural activities not available in Kivikoski. Some discovered that their families' socialist beliefs were a source of harassment, a stumbling block that isolated them on the margins of Canadian society. Their youthful radicalism could become an obstacle when seeking employment or even enlisting in the Canadian army. During the Cold War many moderated their views and disassociated themselves from their own radical past. Others, many of whom perished under Stalinist purges, left to fulfill their parents' dream to build a socialist society in Soviet Karelia. Still others volunteered to fight in the Spanish Civil War. A significant number dedicated their lives to left-wing and progressive causes as union organizers, environmental and peace activists, and feminists. A few have, in later life, even returned to carry on their parents' work in the FOC. Whatever route the second generation chose to travel, their childhood radicalization had imprinted the commitment to social justice deep in their minds.[44] Taimi concluded, "What is the legacy of Kivikoski to me? It is working for the common good. It is accepting responsibility for others. It is fighting for social justice and accepting the strength and equality of women. It is being involved beyond one's own community or even country.

This article was written for Canada, Confederation to Present, *an interactive multimedia history of Canada, a CD-ROM/Web publication, edited by Bob Hesketh & Chris Hackett, Chinook Multimedia, 2001 and has been republished here with permission of Chinook Multimedia and the editors.*

ENDNOTES

[1] The study of the politicization of Ontario farm women has not focused on ethnic communities. Radical Finnish women were not participating in the "mainstream" farmers' organizations such as the United Farmers of Ontario. On farm women, see, for example, Pauline Rankin, "The Politicization of Ontario Farm Women," in *Beyond the Vote: Canadian Women and Politics*, eds. Linda Kealey and Joan Sangster (Toronto:University of Toronto Press, 1998). 10–14.

[2] Linda Kealey, *Enlisting Women for the Cause: Women, Labour, and the Left in Canada, 1890–1920* (Toronto: University of Toronto Press, 1988), 10–14.

[3] Janice Newton, *The Feminist Challenge to the Canadian Left, 1900–1918* (Montreal:McGill-Queen's University Press, 1995); Joan Sangster, *Dreams of Equality: Women on the Canadian Left, 1920–1950* (Toronto:McClelland and Stewart, 1989; Kealey and Sangster, eds., *Beyond the Vote* .

[4] Sangster, *Dreams of Equality*, 239.

[5] For additional information on Finnish immigrant women, see my articles "Finnish Women's Experiences in Northern Ontario Lumber Camps, 1920–1939," and "'I Won't Be a Slave!' Finnish Domestics in Canada, 1911–1930", both in this volume, and my book *Defiant Sisters: A Social History of Finnish Canadian Women 1890–1920*. For a more general account of the Finnish experience in Canada, see my book *From Heroes to Enemies: Finns in Canada, 1937–1947* (Beaverton, Ontario:Aspasia Books, 2000).

[6] Nancy Mattson, ed., *Life in the New Finland Woods* (Rocanville, SK:New Finland Historical Society, 1982). This collection of articles on the local history of New Finland, Saskatchewan, includes information about the lives of Prairie women. Similarly, the Thunder Bay Finnish-Canadian Historical Society has published a settlement history of its rural communities: *A Chronicle of Finnish Settlements in Rural Thunder Bay* (Thunder Bay, Ontario:Thunder Bay Finnish Canadian Historical Society, 1976). Although weak on information on women or analysis in general, the book offers reliable information on the identity and location of early settlers and their communities.

[7] For example, see Nelma Sillanpää, *Under the Northern Lights: My Memories of Life in the Finnish Community of Northern Ontario*, ed. Edward W. Laine (Hull, Quebec:Museum of Civilization, 1994) and Aili Grönlund Schneider, *The Finnish Baker's Daughters* (Toronto:Multicultural History Society of Ontario, 1986).

[8] As is often the case when historians apply feminist methodology, a special bond develops between researcher and subject. During the past year, over the dozens afternoons that Taimi and I spent together, we became friends. In addition, we share many cultural values that may be called "Finnish". We are also both active feminists and interested in women's participation in left-wing politics. All quotes from Taimi are from interviews conducted during 1997 and 1998. Unlike many other subjects, Taimi Davis is articulate, has a good memory, and has kept a rich array of documents. After each interview, she would sit down, sometimes for hours, at her typewriter to record additional details that might be useful. She shared articles, obituaries, and short stories she had written over the years. She gave me newspaper clippings of her family's political activism.

[9] Reino Kero, *Migration from Finland to North America in the Years between the United States Civil War and the First World War* (Vammala, Finland:Vammalan kirjapaino, 1974); Keijo Virtanen, *Settlement or Return? Finnish Emigrants (1860–1920) in the Interwar Overseas Return Migration Movement* (Helsinki, Finland:Suomen hitoriallinen seura, 1979); and Varpu Lindström, *The Finns in Canada* (Ottawa:Canadian Historical Association, 1985).

[10] Marc Metsäranta, ed., *Project Bay Street: Activities of Finnish Canadians in Thunder Bay before 1915* (Thunder Bay, Ontario:Thunder Bay Finnish Canadian Historical Society, 1989), 25–26.

[11] Thunder Bay Finnish-Canadian Historical Society, *A Chronicle of Finnish Settlements*, 7.

[12] Ibid., 182.

[13] Anne Suni, ed. *SS#1 McIntyre & Gorham Kivikoski School Reunion July 29, 1995* (n.p. 1995).

[14] Thunder Bay Finnish-Canadian Historical Society, *A Chronicle of Finnish Settlements*. For example see "Intola," 74–81, "Tarmola," 30–47, "North Branch," 27–30, and "Lappe," 48–59.

[15] Metsäranta, ed., Project Bay Street, 82.

[16] Ibid., 60.

[17] Pirjo Markkola, ed. *Yksi kamari–kaksi sukupuolta: Suomen eduskunnan ensimmäiset naiset* (Helsinki, Finland:Library of Parliament, 1997) and Riitta Jallinoja, *Suomalaisen naisasialiikkeen taistelukaudet* (Porvoo, Finland:Werner Söderström, 1983).

[18] *Canadan Suomalainen Järjestö 25 Vuotta, 1911–1936* (Sudbury, Ontario:Vapaus Publishing, 1936), 38.

[19] *Toveritar*, 29 September 1925 and Metsäranta, ed., *Project Bay Street*, 66.

[20] Suni, ed., *SS#1 McIntyre & Gorham Kivikoski School*.

[21] There is some discrepancy concerning the date of the hall opening. A photograph of the opening of the Kivikoski hall is dated 26 June 1921, but the book *A Chronicle of Finnish Settlements in Rural Thunder Bay* suggests that the hall was built in 1926. The source for this date is an interview. The 1921 date also appears in a typed manuscript which contained photocopied pamphlets, "Festival of Memories," a work prepared by Taimi Davis in June of 1994.

[22] *Vapaus*, 27 February 1930.

[23] "Report from Kivikoski," *Toveritar*, 30 August 1927 and 21 February 1928 and "Report from Finland, Ontario," *Toveritar*, 25 March 1924.

[24] Sangster, *Dreams of Equality*, 29 and Varpu Lindström and Allen Seager, *"Toveritar* and Finnish Canadian Women, 1911–1930," in *Finns in North America: Proceedings from Finn Forum III*, eds. Michael G. Karni, Olavi Koivukangas, and Edward W. Laine (Turku, Finland:Institute of Migration, 1988), 133–153.)

[25] *Toveritar*, 1 March 1927.

[26] *Toveritar*, 23 June 1925.

[27] "Report from Kivikoski," *Toveritar*, 9 April 1929.

[28] *Vapaus*, 21 March 1922.

[29] *Vapaus*, 1 November 1924 and 13 December 1924. The first report gives Lyytinen's age as 15, the second as 16. Taimi Davis to the author, 21 February 1998 and *Vapaus*, 2 March 1926 and 13 March 1926.

[30] Archives of Ontario, Department of Health Records, R.10, 30 A I, "Historical Field Work-Rainy River and Thunder Bay Districts," S.M. Harris, "Report on Summer Work in Thunder Bay, 1925." The reports, prepared by a public health nurse, are dated 25 January 1926.

[31] Sanna Salmijärvi, interview by author, Thunder Bay, Ontario, 1984.

[32] "Report on the Port Arthur District Convention of Delegates Held in Fort William on 25 September 1929," *Toveritar*, 22 October 1929.

[33] "Report of the Port Arthur District Activities," *Työläisnainen*, 4 February 1931.

[34] *Vapaus*, 4 December 1928.

[35] Mauri Amiko Jalava, *"Radicalism or a 'New Deal'?" The Unfolding World View of the Finnish Immigrants in Sudbury, 1882–1932"* (MA thesis, Laurentian University, 1983), especially chapter 12 and *Sudbury Star*, 20 February 1929.

[36] On Finnish lumber workers, see Ian Radforth, "Finnish Radicalism and Labour Activism in the Northern Ontario Woods," in *Nation of Immigrants: Women, Workers, and Communities in Canadian History, 1940s–1960s*, ed. Franca Iacovetta with Paula Draper and Robert Ventresca (Toronto: University of Toronto Press, 1998), 293–316 and Ian Radforth, *Bushworkers and Bosses: Logging in Northern Ontario, 1900–1980*. (Toronto:University of Toronto Press, 1987.)

[37] Satu Repo, "Rosvall and Voutilainen: Two Union Men Who Never Died," *Labour/Le Travailleur* 8/9 (autumn/spring1981/1982): 79–102; Reino Keto, interview by author, Toronto, 1978, Multicultural History Society Collection; and "The Case of the Two Dead Unionists," *Thunder Bay Chronicle*, 24 February 1979.

[38] Sangster, *Dreams of Equality*, 70–71 and Lindström, *Defiant Sisters*, 156–162.

[39] For example see, Varpu Lindström and K. Börje Vähämäki, "Ethnicity Twice Removed: North American Finns in Soviet Karelia," *Finnish Americana* 9 (1992), 14–20; Alexis Pogorelskin, "New Perspectives on Karelian Fever: The Recruitment of North American Finns to Karelia in the early 1930s," *Journal of Finnish Studies* 1:3 (1997), 165–178; Anita Middleton, "Karelian Fever: Interviews with Survivors," *Journal of Finnish Studies* 1:3 (1997), 179–182.

[40] *Sudbury Star*, 4 May 1932.

[41] Martta Laitinen (also known as Lehto), interview by author, Petrozavodsk, Soviet Karelia, 1988 and Varpu Lindström, "Martta Laitinen's Story: Her Work for socialism in Finland, Canada and Soviet Karelia," Canadian Woman Studies/Les cahiers de la femme 10:4 (1989): 68–70.

[42] Anne Walters to Taimi Davis, interview, Toronto, 22 July 1933, Taimi Davis Collection.

[43] "Woman Enters Ward 8 Race," *Toronto Star*, 10 November 1960; "Women Urge Government to Control Food Prices," *Guardian*, September 1973; and "Eläkeläiset vaativat indeksiturvan takaisin," (Pensioners demand back the index protection), *Viikkosanomat*, 24 June 1985.

[44] Interviews with second generation Finnish Canadians who spent their formative years in northwestern Ontario. The indiviaduals interviewed include Wilbert Bohm, Toronto, 1991, Taimi Davis, Toronto, 1997–98, Harold Hietala, Petrozavodsk, 1988, Henry and Osmo Lahti, Vancouver, 1992, Jules Päiviö, Sudbury, 1991, and Paul Siren, Toronto, 1992; the author has also interviewed the current president of the FOC, a second generation woman from northern Ontario, Elsie Jokinen, Toronto, 1996–1998. York University Archives, Varpu Lindström Collection.

Finnish Women's Experience in Northern Ontario Lumber Camps, 1920–1939

> "It was the money all right, that's what drove me to the bush; eventually I even learned to like it there."[1]

Untamed Canadian wilderness held a special attraction for Finns, who were among the first pioneers, trappers, and homesteaders in Northern Ontario communities. Here they found sought-after work in the emerging resource industries and in building the railroads. By the 1920s the lumber industry had become the most important source of livelihood for Finnish men, who began to dominate large sectors of Ontario's pulpwood camps. Many of these lumber workers were newly arrived immigrants. Between 1921 and 1930, more than 37,000 Finns arrived in Canada. Since the very beginning of Finnish immigration to Canada in the late nineteenth century, Ontario has been the favoured destination. In 1931, two-thirds of all Finnish immigrants lived in that province. The majority of the new settlers were men, but by 1931, 11,000 Finnish females (43 percent) had also made Ontario their home.[2]

Finns did not have strong family-chain migration in the fashion of many southern and eastern Europeans and, hence, could rarely rely on financial or housing support from their families. The Finnish "chain" consisted of friends, acquaintances, and, to some extent, siblings. Unlike women of most other nationalities, Finnish immigrant women were universally literate and most of them arrived as single women. As a significant consequence, single women were not restricted by their husband's choices. Many Finnish women, therefore, had considerable independence to choose where they would live and work.[3] Although women were more likely than men to settle in large urban areas of Montreal, Toronto, and Vancouver, the majority still chose to settle in the smaller Finnish communities, especially in Northern Ontario.

The decisions Finnish women made and the experiences they had in Northern Ontario were clearly influenced by their gender, culture, and class. As was the case with all women seeking employment during the 1920s, and especially during the Depression, their options for work were limited. Because they were immigrants, their opportunities were further curtailed by prejudice and by their inability to speak English or French. They were, however, also subject to their own cultural conditioning and value systems. Furthermore, as members of the working class, most did not have the financial resources to acquire professional skills necessary to seek out better-paid occupations. It is within this multi-layered reality that Finnish women tried to carve their place in Canada. Some decided that the best employment opportunities for them were to be found in the lumber camps.

This article will examine the working and living conditions of Finnish women – both single and married—in the Northern Ontario lumber camps by giving voice to the women through extensive use of interviews and letters. It will analyze the economic, social, and political consequences of camp living and will argue that, for some Finnish women, work and life in the lumber camps was a positive experience that offered an opportunity for relatively independent work, self-respect, and some savings, within a protected, ethnically exclusive, and culturally sanctioned environment.

Canadian scholars have found it puzzling to explain how Finnish women gained access to the camp cookhouses "at a time when so few other women entered the traditionally male domain."[4] A closer analysis of their community organization, economic needs, and cultural values will provide some answers. This article will also attempt to determine the extent to which the presence of Finnish women in the lumber camps had any lasting impact on aspects of the Northern Ontario lumber industry.

EMPLOYMENT OPPORTUNITIES

Finnish immigrant women, like Finnish immigrant men, came to Canada primarily for economic reasons. They were, therefore, not only interested in survival but hoped also to save some money. Since Finnish women had little family support, the meager factory wages were simply not enough to pay rent and to support themselves in an urban setting. Hence, they looked for other opportunities more suitable to their specific needs.

By the 1920s, the Finnish communities were well equipped to distribute information about vacancies via employment agencies, newspapers, and, of course, word of mouth. The most common occupation for a Finnish immigrant woman was to be a live-in domestic, but women also worked in a variety of service industries with live-in options such as Finnish-run rooming and boarding houses. These traditionally female occupations had many advantages for the newly arrived immigrant: instant housing, boarding, and an opportunity to learn about the Canadian way of life. Finnish women usually started out as domestics and slowly graduated to "more independent" work. Perhaps the most lucrative legal option, which also provided room and board, was to work in the lumber camps. The only other highly paid options for unskilled immigrant women in Northern Ontario were bootlegging and prostitution.

Although most Finnish women worked first as domestics, some chose to go directly to a lumber camp. One such woman was Martta Laitinen, who described herself as a stubborn, independent, and hardworking woman. She had arrived alone in Sioux Lookout in December 1923. Her husband had left a few months earlier from Finland for Canada, but Martta had no idea where he was. Upon arrival Martta's first priority was to get a job and her second priority was to find her husband. She describes her employment choices: "There were two jobs available, one was to be a dishwasher in a *poikatalo* (men's boarding-house) and the other was to be a dishwasher in a lumber camp." Martta chose the lumber camp. She was not afraid of the dense forest nor the cold climate, both of which were familiar to her from Finland, and she certainly trusted that she could "handle the men."[5]

Martta heard about the jobs by word of mouth, but most would read about them in the Finnish newspapers. The advertisements were designed to attract experienced and hard-working women. Women could be married or single but preferably without children. They had to be willing to work long hours and to sign a long-term commitment to work in a lumber camp. If no work seemed to be available, women would also place their own advertisements. The most opportune time to look for lumber camp work was in August and early September. In August 1923, for example, *Vapaus*, a socialist Finnish Canadian newspaper, ran the following advertisement: "A married woman with years of experience wants to come and work at a lumber camp. A small camp is preferable. My primary objective is cleanliness. Notice! I will not bring children with me."[6]

With the exception of a few Depression years, the demand for Finnish women in the Northern Ontario lumber camps seemed to be greater than the supply. During the 1920s most cultural groups would restrict women's movements. Chaperons were required for single women, and family honour demanded that women not be left alone with men who were strangers. Thus, for women in many southern and east European cultures, work in the lumber camps was simply not an option. For more established Canadian women, work in an isolated camp with "foreigners" was not deemed to be respectable. Finnish women had no such cultural or community-imposed restrictions. They were expected to work hard and to be in charge of their own reputation. Most Finnish women, however, also preferred to stay in the cities and resource towns to enjoy the lively social activities and modern amenities. Work in the lumber camps was not for everyone. It required physical strength, good health, and self-confidence. Women who chose the lumber camp alternative had to believe that the high wages were worth the many personal sacrifices.

LIVING AND WORKING CONDITIONS

Martta Laitinen was satisfied with her working conditions. She did not expect much and she knew in advance that the work would be physically demanding and the living conditions crude and primitive. She liked the men who worked at the camp:

> There were 25 men working at the lumber camp. It was a small lumber camp run by a Finnish man and his wife and they needed a dishwasher... and they wanted a three-month contract for January, February, and March. So I agreed. I was a *tiskari* [dishwasher] and I had to work long days. I started in the morning already at four o'clock and worked till night as they had no other helper. I had to clean the men's camp, the one where they lived, that I cleaned and I had to help the Mrs., she was the cook, and I had to do the dishes and all that other kind of work. The men there were really good, they came at night when I was doing the dishes and they would dry the dishes for me, they would carry wood for me into the kitchen, and the men helped in this way.[7]

The dishwasher worked hard but not as hard as the cooks. Impi Kanerva recalls:

> You had to work hard but at least there was some time off. It was really hard to bring in the supplies for food. We bought nothing ready made. The cook had the worst job. Often the cook had   to   put   the alarm on in the middle of the night to make the dough to be ready to bake bread in the morning. We dishwashers could sleep the night although it still made for a long day. The men were called to breakfast at 6 o'clock. The food was good, you see it was a Finnish camp. We made mountains of cookies.[8]

In the larger camps, the cooks had several people assisting them. After years of working in the bush, Nelma Sillanpää's mother became the head cook of a large lumber camp.

She had to do all the cooking and baking for the camp. She also had a girl to wait on tables and to assist her whenever needed. They had a pump for water over one of the sinks for drinking, washing, and cooking purposes. A chore boy did the dishes, cut the meat, peeled vegetables, and brought in the wood.[9]

Men could put up with cold bunkhouses, pine branches as mat-
tresses, lice, and crowded conditions, but if the food was bad or the
cook inadequate the men would either quit or organize a strike. One
Finnish bush worker, Reino Keto, remembers a rebellion in his camp
because of poor food: "We put on pressure and finally we got so organized that we said if the cook doesn't leave, the men will. We got a
new cook."[10] Another man recalls the very primitive living conditions
but then adds, "The cooks were Finnish women and they made sure,
taking into consideration the circumstances, that the food was pretty
good."

Finnish-Canadian women worked as cooks and dishwashers in the remote
And isolated lumber camps. North of Thunder Bay, 1927.

National Museum of Finland, Sakari Pälsi Collection (VKK 158:44)

Finnish women soon earned a reputation as good cooks and the demand for their services increased with each positive experience. One
reason Finnish cooks were in demand and their food appealed to the
Finnish men is that they cooked familiar ethnic foods. Beans and ba-

con, the standard fare in many lumber camps, was foreign to the Finnish taste. For a newly arrived immigrant the food seemed plentiful—eggs served from large wash basins. William Eklund couldn't believe his ears when he asked how many eggs he could have and the reply was, "Take as many as you want!"[11] After a few years in Canada, Finnish lumber workers learned to demand plenty of meat and potatoes, a variety of soups, such as fish, meat, and pea soup, porridge, pancakes, eggs, and rye bread. In addition, Finns were "addicted to coffee," which was served with *pulla* and cookies.

The women, too, enjoyed the plentiful food in Canadian camps. They even complained about gaining weight. One woman wrote home to Finland, "I am fat as a pig – couldn't get 12 to a dozen – I don't understand why the devil one has to gain so much weight when one first comes to this country."[12] One female camp clerk described the food at a large lumber camp behind Night Hawk Lake:

> The food was wonderful—many kinds of everything. Breakfast at 6 o'clock; most men would make their own lunches, everything was ready for them. Then they'd go into the bush. Those working near the camp would come in for coffee about 10. There was all kinds of goodies, cakes and stuff. There was always quite a few at lunch. All afternoon there was coffee, then supper, and evening coffee. It was really something![13]

Not surprisingly, some woods managers who ranked Finns among the best bush workers in Northern Ontario also complained that "Finns used too much butter and sugar, and cost 15 percent more to feed than French Canadians."[14]

In addition to their ability to cook a variety of tasty dishes in primitive conditions and in large quantities, the Finnish camp women were also praised for their cleanliness. They boasted of having spotlessly clean kitchens, which of course also added to their already heavy workload. One non-Finnish lumber worker explained, "But not a man could stand half up to the Finnish women. God, they even used to scrub the benches that guys sat on."[15] In addition, they tried to take care of their personal appearance. Many camp photographs depict clean, starched, lace-lined aprons and hair done up and covered by nets or white head gear. Although most camps did not have electricity and water had to be carried from nearby streams or wells, Finnish dish-washers were expected to use boiling hot water and to rinse their dishes carefully.

Finnish lumber camps offered bathing facilities. Anna Kauppi heating the *sauna*, north of Sault Ste. Marie, ca 1930.

MHSO, MSR 10887-14

While the conditions in the camps were rough, Finnish women found at least one redeeming factor in the Finnish camps—the *sauna*. According to Ian Radforth, the leading Canadian scholar on Northern Ontario bush workers, Finnish camps were unique in that they offered bathing facilities, and Finnish bush workers gained a reputation for their cleanliness.[16] Linne Korri explains, "Finns always built a *sauna*, the men built it even in non-Finns camps. We [women] heated it up twice a week."[17] An additional benefit of the *saunas* was that they pro-vided convenient and warm laundry facilities. "The women washed clothes at the *sauna* too. A large barrel, which the men filled up, pro-vided the water for laundering."[18] In fact, the availability of a *sauna* became a standard requirement for Finnish women and many Finnish men who worked in the bush.[19]Yrjö Kyllönen, who worked in the lumber camps near Kirkland Lake, makes this point clearly: "I went to another camp but there was no *sauna* or washing facilities so I left!"[20]

Others recalled the democracy and camaraderie in the bunkhouse kitchens. "The kitchen was built so that there would be always room for everyone to eat at once, bosses and men alike, all ate the same food at the same time, sitting around large tables."[21] At night, however, the women were separated from the men. In some camps they slept by the kitchen at one end of the bunkhouse, but at other camps they had their own log building or one that they shared with "the boss."[22] During the afternoon women would sometimes have an hour or two to rest. If they worked in the camps with other women, this was time used for socializing, having a cup of coffee, writing letters, or even going tobogganing. Women found comfort in one another's company, especially since they shared the same language and culture. Relatively speaking, then, the women – dishwashers, cooks, and cookees (cooks' helpers) – enjoyed better living conditions and more privacy than the men. But their working hours were longer. The cooks never had a day off. Rain or shine, the hungry workers had to eat several meals every day of the year.

ECONOMIC OPPORTUNITIES

The hard work and long hours of the lumber camp women were compensated by good wages. Martta Laitinen, for example, was very pleased with her wages as a dishwasher in the winter of 1924. Fifty-five years later she still recalled with pride the size of her paycheque after three months in the lumber camp: "I received a good salary, I got $45 a month and free room and board. So I had over $100 when I left the camp to meet by husband in Vancouver."[23] Similarly Impi Kanerva chose the lumber camp because of its high wages: "I got $80 a month wages as compared to $30 a month in the city as a maid, and that included food and board."

After some experience as dishwashers and cook's helpers, the women graduated to become bakers and cooks and the wages improved significantly. Mary Erickson recalls that before she was married (in the late 1920s or early 1930s) she worked in a lumber camp as a dishwasher and got $35 a month. She adds, "Then I was a cook so I got $75, even $100 [a month]."[24] This possibility for upward mobility and for exceptionally good wages brought women back to the camps year after year despite the heavy work regimen. The larger the camp, the better the wages. Perhaps these perceived economic opportunities are best expressed by Aino Norkooli, a young, single woman who wrote to her sister in Finland from a lumber camp north of Thunder Bay in 1925:

> There are 20 men here and I am here to cook for them....I have one boy as my helper....I get $60 a month wages which is a good salary but I sure have to work hard for it....In the morning I must get up about 5 o'clock and then I run non-stop till 9 o'clock. All the time I have to work and try to bake as much as I can manage....I am trying to learn to become a cook because there is always work   for   them   and good salary. I know even now around here in the camps women get sometimes over $100 a month when they cook for 50 men and that is an excellent salary. And one day I will get it too and then I will come to Finland because I have decided that when I get $300, then I will come to Finland. Maybe I will have it by next spring.[25]

Many factors contributed to the extraordinarily high wages paid to the Finnish lumber camp women. The laws of supply and demand were in women's favour and they had earned a good reputation as clean, capable, and hard-working women. This, however, does not suffice to explain their exceptionally good pay; female cooks could, in fact, earn two or even three times more than the male bush workers. According to statistics compiled by Ian Radforth, cooks during the 1920s earned between $90 and $125 a month and room and board. Such a salary was unheard of for unskilled immigrant women who sought work in the service industries in the urban areas.

Although cooking is traditional female work, cooks in the lumber camps had been exclusively men. When Finnish women began to work as cooks in Northern Ontario camps, they did so on the terms established earlier by male cooks. The common pattern in many occupations women entered between the wars was that wages would decline along with the feminization of the work force. This did not happen in the lumber camps because, throughout the 1920s and 1930s, men continued to dominate in the camps' cookhouses. As long as the women remained in the minority, they were not threatening the position of male cooks. If the Finnish women could work as hard as the men and cook comparable or better meals than the men, their jobs and wages also continued to be set according to the male wage scales.

During the Depression the wages declined, but relatively speaking still offered economic opportunities unattainable in the cities. Aino Norkooli, who was earning $60 in 1925 and expecting to increase her wages to $100 in a few years, wrote home in 1936 that she was working as the only woman in a lumber camp with 25 men and earning $45 a month.[26] According to Radforth, the camp cook's wages were at their lowest in 1932 at $60 a month.[27] Despite the decline in wages, the lumber camps continued to provide women interesting, and relatively well-paid, alternative employment to those willing to put up with the long days, gruelling schedules, primitive living conditions, and isolation.

WOMEN WITH FAMILIES

Sometimes married couples would work in the same camp, the women as dishwashers and cooks and the men as bush workers.[28] This was easier for women who did not have children. Couples often took out contracts and worked in mini camps. In this case they sometimes lived in tents or hastily built small homes.

When on contract there was no time to waste. Artturi Saari's letter describes this well:

> Now we have our own camp. We have six men altogether and one man's Mrs is our cook. We built this camp in the bush, one end of the bunkhouse is for the cook and the other end is for the men. And then we also built a *sauna* (in one day) and now we are building a stable on Sundays so that we don't waste any working days.[29]

Women would also help in the logging, and some wives followed the men into the bush. One woman explained: "It is so good that I enjoy working outdoors. I much rather pull stumps than do the dishes."[30]

Finnish families in the Northern Ontario bush, north of Thunder Bay, 1905.

MHSO, MSR 6891 Part 1 No. 8

In her recent autobiography Nelma Sillanpää describes how many Finnish families lived in the bush cutting pulpwood and adds, "sometimes the women helped, working side by side with their husbands."[31] There is also at least one instance where a woman, Ida Konnila, became a lumber camp operator near Sprucedale and advertised that she was hiring 20 men. She promised them $2 a cord and guaranteed "satisfaction as far as food is concerned."[32]

Camp life posed greater difficulty for women with children. Sometimes mothers would leave their children behind with relatives or with paid babysitters, especially if a child was very young. Boarding, however, was expensive. Aino Norkooli, who left her 11-month-old son in the city, wrote to her mother that the childcare cost $20 while her wages were $45.[33]

Some children grew up in the camps in rather carefree conditions. Their mothers were busy working and the lumber workers didn't have much time for them either. Older children often found the experience a lonely one. One woman recalls: "I had no one with whom to play. So, I always had a pack of cards in my pocket, hoping that someone would play cards with me."[34] Usually there were no schools within traveling distance, so children were sent to board in the cities, where they spent months separated from their parents. Or, like Nelma Sillanpää, they could study independently: "As was the case with most of the children there, I had been enrolled in a correspondence school, I had my lessons to do every day."[35]

Some Finnish families became lumber camp operators. Depending on the size of the operation, the wives either worked as cooks or, if they had the necessary language skills, they could work as clerks in the company store and as bookkeepers for their husbands. The lumber camp clerks were also highly paid, especially in larger camps. Alva Korri remembers when she was a clerk in a camp office after she married: "There was lots of paper work. And you had to sell clothes and things: it's like a little store....I made all of $75 a month. I was offered $65 but I said, 'No I want $75.' And I got it! Ha Ha. We didn't pay for food. I worked for many years. Two years at one camp, three years at another."[36]

Similarly, Irene Hormavirta spent years as a clerk at Algoma Central Mile 155 camp owned by her and her husband. This large lumber camp was a long-term operation and the Hormavirtas built a beautiful log house on the site.[37] Most married women, however, lived in very modest log cabins. Nelma Sillanpää describes her parents' cabin in the woods: "It was a tiny, but warm and cosy cabin. Dad always joked that it was so small that we had to go outside to turn around."[38] During the off-season (summer) the families would return to their small homesteads or to their homes in the cities, but some stayed behind and utilized the empty lumber camps, thus living with their families in remote, isolated cabins all year around. Nelma Sillanpää recalls:

> In June, we traveled by train to another camp still within the beautiful Algoma District. We disembarked near a pile of logs that was marked with a pole showing a mileage number on it. There were many abandoned lumber camps in the area, and anyone could live in them free of charge during the summer months. We were two families....We took the cook camp because it was smaller than the other. The other family

took the men's bunkhouse. The camps were beside a small stream that flowed down the hill to a lake. Across the stream was a sauna.[39]

Thus, lumber camps also offered opportunities for married women. Many Finnish families spent years in the wilderness, sometimes raising their children in the Northern Ontario bush. Ian Radforth cites the case of Nelma Sillanpää's sister-in-law, Elsa Sillanpää, who began working at the age of 15 as a cookee in a lumber camp. The following year she worked in a small camp where she learned to cook. For the next few years she cooked in ever larger camps, increasing her wages accordingly. She then married a bush worker and brought her young children to the camp. When her children grew to school age, she either sent them to town or cooked in a boarding house of a sawmill town. Thus, what often began as seasonal, short-term contract work could stretch into a long, lucrative career and a distinct way of life.

SOCIAL CONDITIONS

Isolation, which often lasted for months, was one of the hardships of lumber camp life. Some Finnish women adjusted to the isolation well, even professed to like it, while others couldn't stand it for long. Unlike in domestic service where Finnish women frequently changed employers, the women who hired themselves out to the camps were expected to sign contracts for the whole season. Many stayed for seven to eight months of the year, while some jobs were year-round. One woman from South Porcupine recalled that the longest stretch she stayed at a camp was nine months, "then I had to see a dentist and I spent a day in town and was back again in the bush....But I didn't mind it at all. You just work and the time passes."[40]

Once again, the great incentive that kept women in isolated camps was money. Hilja Rantala explained in a letter: "I have been already in the bush for four months and things are not easy for me now, but what can I do when I want money so that I could shake off that old country poverty." She added that her bush camp at the time was 198 miles north of the closest major city, Sault Ste. Marie.[41] While the isolation improved the women's economic opportunities and their abilities to save, it could have many psychological and social drawbacks. Minni Lahtinen wrote from Hearst:

> I am one of those children of great misfortune. I buried myself into the dense forest and was quite afraid of people when I came to populated areas. Then I just worked in the lumber camps and I was there many years with hard work and along hours, so I really didn't feel like letting anyone know about me. I had my daughter and son there with me.[42]

Lumber camp cook resting north of Thunder Bay 1927.

VKK 158;14 Sakari Pälsi Collection. National Museum of Finland

Nelma Sillanpää's mother, after a particularly rough season in the woods, "vowed that she would never again go to a logging camp. It was too tough and lonely for a woman." Yet, that summer she was once again cooking for 75 men in a summer lumber camp.[43]

Another cause for concern for the women in the camps was an almost total lack of health care. It could take days to reach the nearest doctor or hospital. Accidents and deaths were quite frequent, and some Finnish women ended their immigration journey in a grave by some remote lumber camp. A particularly sad tale involves a single mother who died in a camp after a short illness. We know about her from the story of her son, Eino Kuusela. This young orphan, who had lived all his life in the lumber camp, was assigned to a Canadian farmer who abused the boy, which led him to escape. He lived alone "like a fox in a hole" in the midst of winter for 76 days before he was apprehended. He had not had any formal education, but he surely had learned the survival techniques required of people living in the wilderness.[44] Sometimes the Canadian press would report lumber camp accidents, such as the story of the scalding of Mrs. H. Saari, a camp cook who was badly burned while lifting a pot of boiling grease off the stove.[45] Mothers with young children were particularly worried about the long distances to doctors and hospitals. It was not uncommon to read about sad accidents to children in the camps.[46] For example, *Vapaus* reported in February 1928: "Eight-month-old little girl burned to death at a lumber camp while her mother was fetching water."[47]

On the positive side, camp life could offer some social advantages, especially for single women, who worked in the male environments. Nowhere were the odds tipped so heavily in women's favour as in the lumber camps. The codes of behaviour were strict: "One did not touch the lumber camp women!" One bush worker remarked that there were "never any shenanigans" and noted that "the girls were treated with respect because they demanded it."[48] Or, as one woman over a hundred years old explained, "No, the men wouldn't touch me. No fooling around in the camps. You couldn't annoy the cook. If the cook left, the camp might have to close." And then she added, "Oh, but how many times I wished that they had!"[49]

With such close proximity, some romances were inevitable as women socialized with men in the camps. Although many complained of being exhausted at night and falling asleep at 9 o'clock during the week, the women would partake in men's social activities on Saturday night and holidays. This included long, political debates, reading, letter-writing, storytelling, and singing. Some would play cards, and, according to one woman, "there was always someone playing the accordion, a Finn worker with his own accordion. He played real nice old Finnish songs."[50]

Alcohol was disallowed at most lumber camps and, overall, the men stayed sober. Occasionally some alcohol was smuggled into the camps, and in remote small bush camps where families worked independently on contract it was not uncommon to find moonshine operations.[51] If fights broke out and rowdiness occurred in the Finnish camps, it was more likely caused by political disagreements than alcohol. "At the camps our entertainment was to argue over politics. If there were Finns, there were Reds and Whites."[52] Unlike in the cities, where the arrival of the lumberjacks after long periods in the bush sometimes erupted in uncontrolled partying, drinking, gambling, and visits to brothels, in the camps the men, by and large, behaved "politely and courteously" towards the women.

Some women were quite calculating about their opportunities. Hilja Rantala wrote from Algoma Central Railway Mile 198 in 1929: "Yes, there would be [suitors] for me too as I am here in the forest cooking for nine men and soon more are coming." But she adds that she has decided to stay single.[53] The fact that women had plenty to choose from was not, by any means, a guarantee of marital bliss, as one woman noted: "There were 60 men to choose from and I chose such a wretched drunk who spent all his money on cards. I had to go back to work to the camps to earn food and clothing for my small children."[54] While lumber camp life could be lonely and isolated, far away from health care, it could also offer women a distinct social advantage.

POLITICAL ACTIVISM

During the 1920s and 1930s the organized, social, cultural, and political activity in Northern Ontario's Finnish communities was dominated by the Finnish-Canadian left. Many lumber workers had arrived
in Canada after Finland's bitter Civil War of 1918, where the "white
army" was victorious. Some had endured persecution and prison camps,
or seen their families and loved ones shot. There were martyrs on both
sides of this fratricidal war and the scars were deep. It was not an easy
task to try to achieve united political action in Canada among people
who were so deeply divided. Yet in the lumber camps the Finns distin-
guished themselves as union organizers. Radforth points out:

> Although the Finnish immigrants dominated the work force in the
> pulpwood camps near Lakehead, up the Algoma Central Railway, and
> along the Canadian Northern Railway west of Sudbury, their participa-
> tion in early unionization drives was far higher than their numbers in
> the industry as a whole. Their activism grew out of the radical, Fin-
> nish-immigrant culture that thrived so vigorously in the north. [55]

There were many kinds of Finnish radicals—"wobblies," socialists,
communists, and social democrats—but during strikes they managed
to pull together to form "united front strike committees."[56]

Finnish men were most active in the Lumber Workers Industrial
Union of Canada (LWIUC); in fact, they were its founders, organizers,
and main supporters. The task of organizing was not easy, but conditions and wages in the camps were so poor and labour practices frequently so dishonest that the men were driven to strike. Northern Ontario was also the scene of many labour battles and bitter strikes between the Finnish-run unions and bush workers and their sometimes
Finnish owners. The most celebrated martyrs of the Finnish Canadian
left are John Voutilainen and Viljo Rosvall, two lumber camp organizers who were allegedly murdered by Finnish anti-union men. According to Radforth, the first of the significant strikes in the Ontario lumber industry occurred in September 1926, and for the next decade
"there was at least one major strike involving several hundred Ontario
lumber workers nearly every year."[57]

Women working in the camps were, of course, affected. During the strike they lost their wages, but often their work continued as they tried to provide soup kitchens to the men manning the picket lines. It seems that many of the women working in the camps were fully supportive of the strikes although aware of and annoyed by the gender inequity within the union movement. Gertie Gronroos, who went to work in a lumber camp kitchen in 1937, remembers with some bitterness that women were not allowed in "those unions," yet women in the kitchen had to go out on strike, without any strike pay, although their conditions didn't improve. "The men got better wages, not us!" She also recalls the hardships caused by the strikes: "Today we don't know what a strike is, you go hungry before you know what a strike is. If the small farmers in the area hadn't brought in supplies, the men would have starved."[58]

Despite the inherent sexism, Finnish women seemed ready to support strikes. *Metsätyöläinen*—a newspaper for Finnish lumbermen—described an attempt to organize a particularly strong anti-union camp north of Port Arthur in 1932. According to the newspaper, the ten-man-strong organizing group had to return to the city without success except for the women. "The cook with her helpers promised to leave."[59]

When union organizers were successful in emptying out the camps, they sometimes made allowances for married couples. Minutes describing a lumber workers' meeting in October 1934 at Algoma Central Railway Mile 122 state: "It was decided that men with families can stay until they can get all of their belonging by the railroad tracks and can in the meanwhile be on picket duty."[60] One reason this was possible was that the women could feed the striking men.

During the strikes most women would return to the Northern Ontario cities and towns where they would become involved in strike support activities and in fund-raising for the strikers: "Before I got married I worked in lumber camps [near Wolf Siding]....My husband belonged to the LWIUC, always we took part in supportive strikes. We had social events at the hall to collect money and equipment for the strikers."[61]

Finnish women's organizations challenged their counterparts to provide funding in an organized fashion. For example, in 1934 the Sudbury Finnish Women's Labour League (WLL) decided to donate $5 to the striking Algoma lumber workers and challenged others to follow suit. "Women of the working class, hurry and fill your obligation [literally, debt of honour]. The lumber workers strike of Algoma must succeed by our united efforts!"[62] Within a few days the Sault Ste. Marie Finnish Women's Labour League decided to follow the example and donate their $5 to the strike fund, and then to publish this decision in a Finnish newspaper and to urge all WLL branches to do the same. "If you have no money, that's no excuse, you must think how to make some." As an example, they cited the efforts of the WLL in Sault Ste. Marie where they had planned to organize an entertainment evening and to give women's handicrafts as door prizes.[63]

Although most of the lumber camp women seem to have shared the men's radicalism and supported their unionizing drives, some did not. In the intolerant political climate, these "white" women could be chased out of the unionized camps. Many camps had their own "committees of investigation," where men would determine whether the newly arrived immigrants were supporters of the working class. One class-conscious Finnish woman complained that women sometimes got away with their conservative political opinions in lumber camps if they were good cooks. She was pleased to report, however, that just recently they had fired an experienced camp cook "because she had cooked for the white army in Finland."[64]

Organizing, striking, and fund-raising helped to consolidate the women's class consciousness, but at the same time these activities also revealed the sexism inherent in the labour movement and in the Finnish radical organizations.

CONCLUSION

Of the limited options available to working-class immigrant women in Northern Ontario, the lumber camps made sense on many levels:

they offered food, housing, a culturally familiar environment, and an opportunity to earn unusually high wages. Because this traditional female work was done mainly by men in most lumber camps, women were able to argue for equal wages. Unlike wages in most other occupations that women entered after World War I, the lumber camp wages remained high and at par with male wages. Lumber camp women, especially if they were cooks and had no family obligations, could indeed achieve their economic goals and save money.

Lumber camp life, however, was clearly not for all women. Only independent, strong, and healthy women survived in the camps. They had to be familiar with cold winters and dense forests and be able to put up with months of isolation. They had to be able to make their own decisions and be free of culturally imposed restrictions on women's mobility. For such women the camps offered a unique lifestyle, where women enjoyed considerable respect, some social advantages, and, at times, found themselves in positions of power. Camps could simply not function without the cooks. The work was clearly demanding, even gruelling, at times dangerous, and isolation could take its toll. The negative aspects of camp life, however, could be partially alleviated because the Finnish women worked almost exclusively within the cultural safety of Finnish lumber camps and in many camps enjoyed the camaraderie of other Finnish women and men.

Within these camps the Finnish women raised the standards of food and cleanliness and had an overall civilizing impact on camp life. As a result, many men, as they moved from camp to camp, began to expect and demand similar standards in non-Finnish camps. It is no surprise then, that in addition to wages, unions began to pay increasing attention to living conditions. Women also made a significant contribution by supporting the many lumber workers' strikes, some of which were successful. Thus, it can be argued that the presence of the Finnish women in the camps had an impact on the living and working conditions of the camps that reached far beyond the particular camps where they happened to work.

120   Varpu Lindström

Finally, as the first women in the bush camps, Finns pioneered the way for other women who wished to work in Northern Ontario lumber camps. After World War II, when camp life gradually became modernized and conditions improved, women from many cultural groups sought work in the camps. By then, the presence of women in the camps was no longer a novelty but often an expectation. The path for the lumber camp jobs had been cleared and the standard set by Finnish immigrant women.

This article was originally published in Changing Lives – Women in Northern Ontario *edited by Margaret Kechnie and Marge Reitsmastreet, Dundurn Press, Toronto & Oxford, 1996. Article reprinted with permission from Dundurn Press Ltd/INORD. Copyright 1996.*

ENDNOTES

[1] Interview with Aina Mackie by Varpu Lindström, Vancouver, B.C., 1982.
[2] Varpu Lindström-Best, *The Finns in Canada* (Ottawa: Canadian Historical Association, 1985), p. 7, p. 16; Varpu Lindström, *Defiant Sisters: A Social History of Finnish Immigrant Women in Canada 1890–1930* [Toronto: Multicultural History Society of Ontario (MHSO), 1992], pp. 34–39.
[3] Finnish emigration patterns have been discussed in Reino Kero, *Migration from Finland to North America in the Years Between the United States Civil War and the First World War* (Turku: The Migration Institute, 1974); in Keijo Virtanen, *Settlement or Return: Finnish Emigrants (1860–1930) in the International Overseas Return Migration Movement* (Turku: The Migration Institute, 1979); and in Lindström, *Defiant Sisters*, pp. 1–39. On chain migration, see, for example: Franc Sturino, *Forging the Chain: Italian Migration to North America 1880–1930* (Toronto: MHSO, 1990); and Franca Iacovetta, *Such Hardworking People: Italian Immigrants in Postwar Toronto* (Kingston: McGill-Queen's University Press, 1992), pp. 3–51.
[4] Ian Radforth, *Bushworkers and Bosses: Logging in Northern Ontario 1900–1980* (Toronto: University of Toronto Press, 1987), p. 101.
[5] Interview with Martta Laitinen by Varpu Lindström and Börje Vähämäki, Petroskoi, Russia, 1988.
[6] *Vapaus*, 21 August 1923; Lindström, *Defiant Sisters*, p. 86.
[7] Interview with Martta Laitinen, 1988.
[8] Interview with Impi Kanerva by Lennart Sillanpää, Schumacher, Ont., MHSO ILF 1925.
[9] Nelma Sillanpää, *Under the Northern Lights: My Memories of Life in the Finnish Community of Northern Ontario,* ed. Edward W. Laine (Ottawa: Canadian Museum of Civilization, 1994), p. 24.
[10] Interview with Reino Keto by Varpu Lindström, Toronto, 1978. MHSO ILF 5187.
[11] Interview with William Eklund by Lennard Sillanpää, Sudbury, 1977. MHSO ILG 2222.
[12] American Letter Collection (ALC), University of Turku, KAR:CXXXI, Hilja Rantala, 2 March 1929, AC Ry. Mile 198.
[13] Interview with Alva Korri by Lennard Sillanpää, Porcupine, Ont., 1977. MHSO ILG 1164.
[14] Radforth, *Bushworkers and Bosses*, p. 33.
[15] Radforth, *Bushworkers and Bosses*, p. 101. Quote by Buzz Lein.
[16] Radforth, *Bushworkers and Bosses*, pp. 92–93.

[17] Interview with Linne Korri by Lennard Sillanpää, Timmins, 1977. MHSO ILF 1921. See also the interview with Alva Korri, 1977.

[18] Nelma Sillanpää, *Under the Northern Lights*, p. 9.

[19] Wm Eklund, *Canadan Rakentajia: Canadan Suomalaisten Järjestön Historia vv. 1911–1971*, (Toronto: Vapaus Publishing, 1983), p. 106.

[20] Interview with Yrjö Kyllönen by A-M Lahtinen, Sudbury, 1978. MHSO ILG 2904.

[21] Interview with Linne Korri, 1977.

[22] Interview with Yrjö Kyllönen, 1978.

[23] Interview with Martta Laitinen, 1988.

[24] Interview with Mary Erickson by Raili Nieminen and Helena Doherty, Nolalu, Ont., 1979. MHSO ILF 7458.

[25] ALC, University of Turku, Finland, EURA:XXI, Aino Norkooli to A. Hägerman, 15 December 1925 in "dense forest."

[26] ALC, University of Turku, Finland, EURA:XXI, Aino Norkooli to her mother in Finland, 27 October 1936 in "at the camp."

[27] Radforth, *Bushworkers and Bosses*, p. 255.

[28] Eklund, *Canadan Rakentajia*, p. 109.

[29] ALC, University of Turku, LOIM:XXXIII, Artturi Saari, 17 September 1929, "at a bush camp."

[30] ALC, University of Turku, MER:CCVIII, Raakel Vanhala, 30 May 1946, Sault Ste. Marie, Ont.

[31] Nelma Sillanpää, *Under the Northern Lights*, p. 6.

[32] *Vapaus*, 12 August 1922.

[33] ALC, Aino Norkooli, 1936.

[34] Nelma Sillanpää, *Under the Northern Lights*, p. 26.

[35] Nelma Sillanpää, *Under the Northern Lights*, p. 14.

[36] Interview with Alva Korri, 1977.

[37] Interview with Irene Hormavirta by Varpu Lindström, Toronto, 1978. MHSO ILF 4985.

[38] Nelma Sillanpää, *Under the Northern Lights*, p. 7.

[39] Nelma Sillanpää, *Under the Northern Lights*, p. 12.

[40] Interview with Alva Korri, 1977.

[41] ALC, Hilja Rantala, 1929.

[42] ALC, University of Turku, EURA:XXII, Minni Lahtinen, Hearst, Ont., 1961.

[43] Nelma Sillanpää, *Under the Northern Lights*, p. 25.

[44] Varpu Lindström, *Uhmattaret: Suomalaisten siirtolaisnaisten vaiheita Kanadassa 1890–1930* (Helsinki: WSOY, 1991), p. 132.

[45] *Daily Times Journal*, 30 September 1930 as quoted by Nancy Chong Johnson's unpublished undergraduate research paper "Finnish Immigrants in Thunder Bay: Representation in the English-Language Press 1875–1878, 1903–1906, 1930" (Toronto: University of Toronto, Finnish Studies Program, 1995).

[46] Lindström, *Defiant Sisters*, pp. 86-87; for additional information on children in the lumber camps, see Lindström, *Uhmattaret*, pp. 131-33.

[47] *Vapaus*, 2 February 1928.

[48] Radforth, *Bushworkers and Bosses*, p. 102.

[49] Interview with Aina Mackie, 1982.

[50] Interview with Alva Korri, 1977.

[51] Ian Radforth, "Finnish Lumber Workers in Ontario, 1919–1946," *Polyphony* 2 (Fall, 1981), p. 26; Nelma Sillanpää, *Under the Northern Lights*, pp. 10–11.

[52] Interview with Toivo Tienhaara by Lennard Sillanpää, South Porcupine, Ont., 1977. MHSO ILF 1161; Radforth, "Finnish Lumber Workers," p. 26.

[53] ALC, Hilja Rantala, 1929.

[54] Interview with Martta Huhtala by Varpu Lindström, Parry Sound, Ont., 1983. York University Archives, Varpu Lindström collection.

[55] Radforth, *Bushworkers and Bosses*, p. 108.

[56] Radforth, "Finnish Lumber Workers," p. 29.

[57] Radforth, "Finnish Lumber Workers," p. 29.

[58] Interview with Gertie Gronroos by Helena Doherty, Port Arthur, Ont., n.d. (1978?). MHSO ILF 7198.
[59] *Metsätyöläinen* 8 (1932): p. 15
[60] *Industrialisti,* 11 October 1934.
[61] Interview with Mary Erickson, 1979.
[62] Unidentified Finnish language newspaper clipping, 17 October 1934.
[63] Unidentified Finnish language newspaper clipping, 29 October 1934.
[64] *Vapaus,* 26 February 1921; Lindström, *Defiant Sisters,* p. 87.

Propaganda and Identity Construction:

Media Representation in Canada of Finnish and Finnish-Canadian Women during the Winter War 1939–1940

Small ethnic groups in Canada have rarely been at the centre of media attention. If they have found their activities described in major Canadian dailies, the news has usually been negative or sensational in nature. During the Depression, the Finns, like many other European immigrants in Canada, grew accustomed to bad press about their community. The media reported on arrests of radical labour leaders, trials of Finnish strikers, demonstrators, communists, newspaper editors, and deportation cases – and they did so in ways that demonized left immigrant workers as "dangerous foreigners."[1] Such lopsided coverage hardly increased Canadians' understanding of ethnic communities nor did it provide useful information about the countries of origin.

Wars inevitably call into question the loyalty of citizens and place immigrants under special scrutiny. Many of those deemed to be a threat to the government's war efforts – pacifists, left-wing radicals, and enemy nationals—had their civil liberties curtailed.[2] If, in addition, they belonged to so-called visible minority groups, they became "objects of scorn."[3] Considering this background, one might well imagine how stunned Finns in Canada were by the overwhelmingly favourable coverage by the Canadian media of Finland and Finnish

Canadians during the Winter War, which raged from 30 November
1939 until 13 March 1940. Triggered by a Soviet invasion into Finland
and characterized by truly ferocious fighting, the Winter War that pitted Finns against Russians captured the imagination of the media. Almost instantly, the Canadian media was "drenched with sympathy" for
the small nation of Finland. Newspapers depicted the war as a battle
between David and Goliath, the underdog and the bully, the small
"gallant and heroic" nation of lawabiding and civilized people against
the "barbarous," "greedy," Communist Russians.[4]

During the more than one hundred days of intense press coverage
of the Winter War, the media also discovered the "Finnish woman"
and, indeed, actively promoted various constructions of this female
ethnic subject. This photo essay explores the media manipulation of
the "Finnish woman" and how it served a variety of different propaganda agendas. Such manipulation was a complex and multilayered
process: the Finnish woman's race and the many gendered roles she
played made her a malleable role model, an ideal sister to heterosexual
Anglo-Canadian women—at least during a particular historical moment.

An understanding of the Canadian media's glorification of these
female strangers requires us to look briefly at the events during the
first year of the Second World War. When Canada declared war on
Germany on 10 September 1939, the initial flurry of wartime activity,
recruitment, patriotic speeches, and the creation of new enemy aliens
in the country, captured the lion's share of media attention. But as
these early dramatic events soon gave way to what became known as
the "phony war" (when little happened on the European battle front),
the lack of action in Europe meant few exciting stories for war correspondents. According to Canadian military historian J.L. Granatstein,
early wartime activity had "stagnated, degenerating to a battle of leaf-
lets and loudspeakers across the Rhine."[5] All this changed, however,
when the Soviet Union attacked Finland on 30 November 1939. Suddenly the world became witness to an active theatre of war replete with
heroes and enemies, bombed-out cities, suffering civilians, and soldiers ambushed and frozen in the battle between "mighty Russia and

the tiny nation of Finns." The Winter War became front-page news as Finns fought against Canada's ideological enemy—Communist Russia – for democracy and independence. Canadian war correspondents were dispatched to the Arctic front. Day after day, bold headlines trumpeted the message of the small heroic nation's dogged determination to defend its borders. The media reported stunning successes of the Finnish Army against formidable odds: "Finns Drive Russians from Petsamo, Soviet 'Parachute Army' Wiped Out; Russians' Losses Soar as Retreat Continues Along Three Sectors; Russians Lose 100,000 Men and 300 Tanks; Finns Smash Invader on Four Fronts, Annihilate Flower of Russian Army." Characteristic of the media coverage of the Winter War was the following depiction: "Pitted against Finn supermen Russians flounder hopelessly in deep drifts of arctic forest."[6] Inspired Canadians flocked to volunteer to fight the Russians alongside the "Finn supermen." An influential committee, headed by Senator Arthur Meighen, recruited the volunteers and raised funds for the Finnish war effort. Canadian military leader Col. Hunter announced that two thousand Canadian volunteers were ready to leave for Finland on 14 March 1940.[7]

And then, almost as suddenly, came the announcement that an armistice was declared on 13 March 1940. Canadians were perplexed. What they had read in the newspapers or heard on the radio had not prepared them for an armistice, let alone for the heavy territorial losses suffered by Finland. Furthermore, as the hostilities ceased, the fate of the Finns soon became yesterday's news. In the spring and summer of 1940, the media attention shifted to the new and disturbing developments in Europe as Hitler's successful *Blitzkrieg* began conquering one democratic country after another. On 22 June 1941, Hitler attacked the Soviet Union and four days later, Finland, alongside Germany, followed suit. Intent on reclaiming its lost territory, Finland was now a co-belligerent of Germany, which in turn, prompted the Canadian government, on 7 December 1941, to declare Finland an enemy of Canada. Finns in Canada thus became enemy aliens. Thereafter, if the Finns received any press coverage at all, they were depicted as tired, reluctant soldiers fighting on the wrong side. The "barbaric" Russians had now become valuable allies. As this brief summary suggests, the window of opportunity for this study is small indeed. The positive media coverage began during late summer 1939, as war clouds gathered over Europe, followed by a groundswell of coverage during the Winter War, which then waned soon after the armistice was declared.

These changing contexts shaped in fundamental ways the portrayal of Finnish people, including women, in Canada and their changing status as sisters or strangers. During the summer of 1939 the government of Finland provided the North American press with photos designed to depict a nation of civilized, healthy, athletic, and beautiful people. Initially, this propaganda was part of an advertising campaign to entice Canadians to travel to the summer Olympics to be hosted by Helsinki in 1940. By the fall, the focus shifted to describing a small, brave nation in need of support, and Finnish state propaganda emphasized the role of women in nation-building, their crucial role in preparing Finland's defences, and later their role in Finland's war effort.[8]

Canada recognized the potential need to recruit women to bolster its own war effort. The intense attention given to the activities of the Finnish women at the beginning of the war foreshadowed the later wartime propaganda in Canada intended to recruit women *en masse*. Finnish sisters were deemed suitable heroines and role models for Canadian women. After all, they were fighting on the "right" side against Canada's—and democracy's—ideological enemy, the Communist Soviet Union. Stories of Finnish women served as positive examples of how women became critical contributors to the war effort while still maintaining their "womanhood."[9] At the same time, the Finnish-Canadian community, which numbered more than 41,000 in 1941, quickly seized on the opportunities offered by this exceptional period of the glorification of everything Finnish. Community members, especially those belonging to nationalist and religious organizations, plotted how best they could get their own message across. They wanted the media to cover their assurances of their continuing loyalty to Canada while raising funds in aid of the Finnish war effort. More significantly, the Winter War presented an unparalleled opportunity for Finnish Canadians to have their voices heard across Canada. Finnish-Canadian women were willing participants in the community's propaganda efforts and in the creation of an idealized "Finnish woman". It also offers a dramatic illustration of how "ethnic nationalism" can be gendered.

The representation of the Finnish woman during this period of crisis had many and seemingly contradictory layers. The mythical Finnish woman who appeared on the pages of the major Toronto and Montreal English-language newspapers was at once objectified as a beautiful woman, an aggressive soldier, a sacrificing "traditional" mother and wife, a strong peasant or construction worker, and an emancipated and independent woman. She was a victim and an initiator, supportive and demanding, weak and powerful. In other words, she represented the underlying ferment of Canadian women's changing roles in society, the simmering challenges to their sexual identities and the increasing dissatisfaction with the unequal economic and political power of women. The many different constructs of Finnish women co-existed in harmony and went uncontested on the pages of Canada's leading newspapers.

Why, one might ask, were the Finnish women deemed suitable role models? One reason may be that they were distant and strange enough not to pose any immediate threat. So little was known about Finland that fact and fiction about its women could safely mingle. Indeed, erroneous and often sensationalist reports went without protest. Another reason may be that a Eurocentric and often racist press found Finnish women eminently acceptable. They were white and belonged to the northern race; in fact, the press never tired of pointing out just how "fair" or "blonde" they were. They were also Protestant, Western in habits, and relatively well educated. In other words, mainstream Anglo-Canadian women could conceivably identify with their newly found Finnish heroines who stood beside—not behind—their men. Drawing on the coverage and especially images of Finnish women to appear in several English-Canadian newspapers during the period under review, the following sections examine the seven complex images of Finnish women that emerged in the Canadian media. These were the traditional woman, the beautiful blonde, the worker, the emancipated woman, the woman in the Lotta Svärd auxiliary, the soldier, and the immigrant woman as fundraiser.

THE TRADITIONAL WOMAN

The national costume of Finnish women became an important propaganda weapon and a symbol of traditional peasant way of life. National costumes caught the attention of the reader and many of the captions that accompanied the numerous photos had a didactic quality to them. Identifying images of Finnish peasant women at work, for example, were captions that informed the Canadian public that notwithstanding the "peculiar" costumes worn by Finnish women they really were just like Canadian women. In reality, women in Finland never wore national costumes, except on very special holidays or when performing traditional folk dances or songs on stage. Indeed, most women never owned the colourful ceremonial outfit, which was made of wool, cotton, intricate lace, and worn with heavy bronze or silver jewelry. Although hardly an outfit suitable for daily routines, press photographs released by the Finnish government suggested otherwise. They frequently portrayed women in these costumes. Four photographs published in the *Toronto Star* on 5 December 1939 are emblematic. The first photograph shows a young woman in national costume weaving; the second one has ten women in national costumes surrounding an old bearded man who looks like a traditional rune singer of Finnish mythological songs. The third image portrays a Sami woman and the text draws attention to her costume: "Lapland girls have their own peculiar dress." The fourth is a picture of a stout peasant woman baking, with the explanation: "Peasant women maintain the old-fashioned way of cooking." In stark contrast to these peaceful, though exotic, photographs of women in their most traditional roles is the bold caption: "Women of Finland Stand Beside Their Men" and "They Live and Fight in Traditional Style."[10]

WOMEN IN FINLAND STAND BESIDE THEIR MEN

THEY LIVE AND FIGHT IN TRADITIONAL STYLE

Finland also sent photographs meant to depict the "typical" Finnish women, and some of them also contain images of women wearing a national costume—including one of a young Finnish mother holding her impeccably dressed plump child. The caption reads: Typical of the hardy, vigorous and purposeful character of the Finns is this peasant mother and child."[11] Similarly, the *Montreal Standard* carried a large photograph of two young maidens, dressed in the national costume who were described as "typical of Finland."[12]

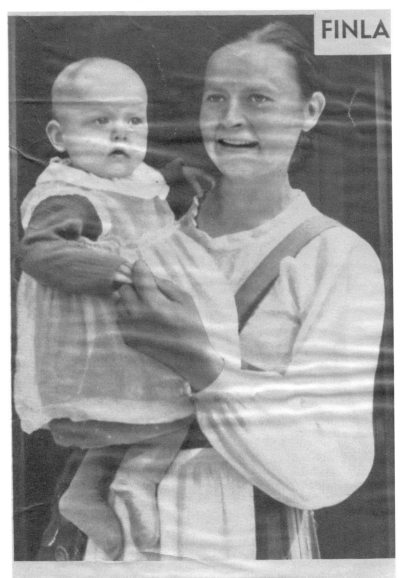

TYPICAL OF THE HARDY, vigorous and purposeful character of the Finns is this peasant mother and child (above). At right, Fanni Luukkonen, head of the Lotta Svard organization of over 100,000 women, whose members will step into vital jobs in wartime

THE BEAUTIFUL BLONDE

The construction of the beautiful, mythical, healthy, and, again, exotic Finnish woman took many forms. One of the first such stories that dwelt on this theme in the Canadian press appeared on 10 November 1939, when Birgit Kansanen, "a pretty Finnish student studying at the University of Toronto" was interviewed for the *Toronto Star*. This "student" had in fact been supervisor of nursing for the Red Cross in northern Lapland. Her life, which was hardly typical of Finnish women, was described in exciting and daring terms. Her skiing trips through the wilderness and forests of Lapland to reach remote communities are depicted as heroic. Far above the Arctic Circle, in the darkness of the northern winter, she was pulled in sleighs by reindeer and sheltered from blizzards by her St. Bernard dog. Far from being a passive female subject, Kansanen assisted the media by providing details of her lonely and brave struggles against the elements. At one point, she described being "caught in a snowstorm without [matches] and I slept beside my St. Bernard dog all night to keep from freezing." Kansanen's story is exceptional indeed. Most Finnish women would have only seen reindeer in a zoo and few would have traveled alone in a blizzard through the vast wilderness. This dramatic story was accompanied by a photograph of smiling Birgit Kansanen.[13]

On 9 December 1939, the *Montreal Standard* published in its weekly magazine several pages of photographs of Finland depicting Finnish cultural heroes, Finnish architecture, and the Finnish landscape. Included is also a special section on "Finland's Women." One of its captions, referring to a photograph of two blonde girls leaning against a log cabin, tells the reader that "Finnish Girls Are Fair." It then elaborates further: "Typical of Finland are these happy country girls with their long fair hair, broad foreheads, and strong white teeth." Another page is dominated by a smiling, saluting Tuulikki Paananen. The caption, while misspelling her name, refers to her as "Finland's leading screen star." The popular photograph of Paananen, who spent the war years in Hollywood, was featured again on 30 December 1939 in the *Toronto Star Weekly*.

FINNISH GIRLS ARE FAIR

TYPICAL OF FINLAND are these happy country girls with their long fair hair, broad foreheads and strong white teeth. Four-fifths of the population live in the country, only one fifth in cities.

TYPICAL OF FINLAND are these happy country girls with their
long fair hair, broad foreheads and strong white teeth.

TUULIKI PAANEN above is Finland's leading screen star.

This time her photograph filled the entire page.[14] Needless to say, not all Finnish women were fair, strong, or healthy, and only the exceptional few ever became Hollywood stars.

THE WORKER

In stark contrast to the smiling beauties in national costumes are the strong women engaged in heavy manual labour. A factory worker included in a special *Star Weekly* photo coverage entitled "Finland Resists Threat to Her Independence," was described as "a sturdy girl worker in a paper-board factory." The woman in the picture, looking directly into the camera, is wearing loose overalls with rolled-up shirt sleeves, and she is carrying a heavy load of paper boards. A picture on the same page shows five stout, elderly women crouching with brushes over a cobblestone street. Described as Finnish women street cleaners,

the caption told readers that "their conscientious scrubbing of pavements...and the feminine thoroughness they bring to such jobs in other
walks of life have given Finland the reputation of the cleanest country
in Europe." For many readers it undoubtedly required quite a stretch of
imagination to associate these stout, elderly street scrubbers with
"feminine" attributes, though they might well have got the message
that in Finland women could perform all kinds of heavy labour.[15]

ABOVE are Finnish women street cleaners. Their conscientious scrubbing of pavements and sidewalks and the feminine thoroughness they bring to such jobs in other walks of life have given Finland the reputation of the cleanest country in Europe. Right: A sturdy girl worker in a paper-board factory.

ABOVE are Finnish women street cleaners. Their conscientious scrubbing of pavements and sidewalks and the feminine thoroughness they bring to such jobs in other
walks of life have given Finland the reputation of the cleanest country in Europe.
Right: A sturdy girl worker in a paper-board factory.

Women Behind Finland's Lines

The large number of women in heavy industries was partially due to Finland's legislation of compulsory labour laws for all healthy Finns, eighteen to fifty-five years of age that was enacted in October 1939 in anticipation of the war. Once the war started, the war industries were in desperate need of workers. Indeed, during the war more than half the people working in Finland's war industries were women.[16] Some parallels were drawn with the British women's war effort as young girls and women were organized to do a variety of jobs "behind the lines." Two photographs show "a group of girls making window blinds for blackouts at night." The women "aided by a lone man" are "adept with tools." Another photograph is of a roomful of women busily at work preparing bandages. The caption states: "Standing by – Women in Finland were as resolute as their men in demanding independence."[17] Canada, too, anticipated the need to recruit housewives into war industries. Many immigrant women who were originally recruited into the low-paying domestic service sector found new employment opportunities in war industries. Finnish-Canadian domestics were quick to follow the example set by women in their homeland and changed their aprons to overalls and their small pay-cheques to "men's wages."[18]

The stories and photo images of Finnish women workers happily doing "men's work" while maintaining their "femininity" helped set the stage for the later strong recruitment of Canadian women into the war industries. For this purpose the federal government established the Women's Voluntary Service Division in 1941. As the labour shortage became critical in Canada, the Women's Division of the Selective Service agency carried out a national registration in 1942 of all women aged twenty to twenty-four.[19]

THE EMANCIPATED WOMAN

Finnish government propaganda wished to create the image of a modern, emancipated woman who could stand next to the traditional woman. Educational material proudly proclaimed the positive, even enviable, position of women in Finland. And some Canadian newspapers, as the following excerpt shows, quoted it at length:

> In Finland women take their places alongside their menfolk in every walk and profession from the highest to the lowest. Granted the vote in 1906 when their sisters in other countries were only just beginning to think about such things they have carried on from there and one of their

number, a domestic servant named Miina Sillanpää was elected one of the first women deputies and worked her way to a cabinet post.[20]

First-wave feminist and suffrage leader Nellie McClung joined the chorus of praises of the emancipated Finnish woman, pointing out, for instance, that they had received the right to vote eleven years before their Canadian sisters. McClung became interested in Finnish women through her own Finnish domestic servant; the protagonist in her novel *Painted Fires* was a stubborn and independent Finnish maid. In a lengthy article about the war in Finland, McClung reinforced this image of emancipated Finnish women, and also described women's independent role in the Lotta Svärd "women's unit of defense." But she also declared that Finnish women were "just like ourselves," and, as supporting evidence, noted that "Finnish women have many societies, including the YWCA and the National Council of Women, both affiliated with the international bodies."[21]

In short, Canadian press coverage gave the impression that Finnish women enjoyed equality with Finnish men. In reality, of course, they earned much less than men, were less likely to find themselves in leadership positions, and have yet today to reach equal pay or equal representation in the parliament.

WOMEN'S AUXILIARY: THE LOTTA SVÄRD

Many references in articles, interviews, and photographs were made to the Lotta Svärd organization and its uniformed women soldiers. The main impression gleaned from the newspaper coverage is of an organization for all Finnish women, that its members were "conscripted" and that they served both as an auxiliary and as a fighting force. The press carried an unusual image of elderly, stern, and important-looking Finnish women in grey military uniforms seated in a meeting, holding documents in their hands, while a large portrait of Marshall Mannerheim hangs behind them, thus presenting an authoritative and respectful image of the women in Finland's Lotta Svärd. One of the women is identified as Fanni Luukkonen, the head of the 100,000-member organization. These were not young women looking for adventure but mature women with serious wartime business on their hands.

Fanni Luukkonen, head of the Lotta Svard organization of over 100,000 women, whose members will step into vital jobs in wartime.

Finnish women were portrayed as most eager and willing participants in the activities of the Lotta Svärd. Under the title "Women Rush to Serve," for example, the *Toronto Star Weekly* told readers the following:

> Stenographers whose jobs were wiped out by the war have rushed into Red Cross canteen work in Finland's splendid auxiliary, the Lotta Svärd. Finnish women are now serving 10 to 15 hours a day for the country's freedom. This is little Finland, unflinching and undaunted before the mighty Soviet Goliath which threatens its life.[22]

—Associated Press Wirephoto

SHE WATCHES AND WHEN RAIDERS COME THE FINNS ARE READY

Essential to Finland's weak air defences are the services of this girl (LOWER). From her observation post she scans the skies. When from her vantage point among the trees she sights raiding planes, she signals the defences and the air-raid alarms are sounded. Gunners, forewarned. are at their stations and with good marksmanship bring down enemy craft.

The text accompanying four pictures of quintessentially "traditional"-looking Finnish women in national costumes declares that "Women of Finland Stand Beside their Men," and then offers the following examples:

> Household Crafts such as the weaving this girl is doing have been forsaken for more active service now that Finland is at war. Girls and women have been trained in the part they must play in defence of their homeland. Like the women of Britain, they are now engaged in air raid precaution and army auxiliary work.[23]

Yet, the Lotta Svärd organization was far from an inclusive female organization. On the contrary, it was a political auxiliary organization for conservative Finnish women. It had strict screening procedures and only admitted as its members right-wing, mainly middle-class "Christian and moral" women. The organization was founded immediately after Finland's civil war in 1919, which had pitted "red" Finns against the conservative "white" Finns. It originated as an auxiliary force to the conservative government's Civil Guard by women who had participated on the side of the "White Guard" against the "Red Guard". When the Winter War broke out, the Lotta Svärd had an elaborate network of what they called "reputable women" ready to serve in auxiliary roles. Decidedly anti-Communist, the organization did not allow left-wing Finnish women to join, and only after the Second World War did it agree to co-operate with women from Social Democratic organizations. It was thus seriously misleading to suggest that "all" Finnish women flocked to join the Lotta Svärd, but an impressive number did. During the Winter War, about 90,000 Lottas were mobilized. About 25,000 of them worked within the war zone, where they served in the field kitchens (11,000), took care of supplies (3,500), stood on guard in some 650 air defence locations (3,000), provided medical services (2,500), and clerical services (2,000). An additional 6,100 nurses worked through the Red Cross in the field hospitals. The example of a well-organized, uniformed, female defence unit engaged in important auxiliary work in aid of Finland's war effort, could serve as an appropriate model for Canadian women.

THE SOLDIER

Some articles and photographs give the impression that Finnish women were not only serving behind the lines or in auxiliary roles but were an integral part of the army, fighting as soldiers on the battlefield. Photographs depict uniformed "female members of Finland's army on an observation post high in a tree." Another uniformed woman peers through her binoculars: "She watches and when raiders come the Finns are ready." The caption assures the reader that "Essential to Finland's weak air defences are the services of this girl."[24]

Finnish women were also described as fierce gun-carrying soldiers. A bizarre article, which went uncontested, gives an image of a fully mobilized army of women. A section of the article, based on an interview with Mary Lehtonen of Toronto, sports the subheading, "Women Better Fighters." It deserves to be quoted at length:

> "Wait until the Russian soldiers come face to face with a regiment of determined Finnish women soldiers," advised Mary Lehtonen today. This 19-year old girl has just returned from a two-month visit to the homeland and claims, from what she saw of the war preparations, that the women of Finland are more daring than the men. "I saw whole regiments of women digging trenches along the Russian-Finland border. They worked side-by-side with the men and are trained to shoulder a gun if necessary. If that does happen, the Russians had better look out," said Ms Lehtonen grimly. "Our men are good fighters but our women are better"…"From past experience in war," Ms Lehtonen continued, "we know that our enemies are more afraid of the women than men."[25]

The Winter War became famous for the Finnish ski troops which swiftly ambushed the enemy during the exceptionally cold and snowy winter. Canadians were told that women were part of the ski troops. A headline above a uniformed woman on skis says "Draft Women to Fight Reds." The *Globe and Mail* identifies her as "[o]ne of [the] Finnish women who has been drafted for army service as ski-troops." The article continues, "The Finns have reported many successful attacks by their silently gliding ski troops in surprise attacks on the invading Russians."[26] A Finnish-Canadian woman, Aili Laatunen, declared, "I think it is the sacred duty of every man and woman to fight for his country when that country is attacked."[27] Despite media reports to the contrary, Finnish women did not carry arms or join the army as soldiers during the Winter War. Only at the end of the Second World War in 1944 did the Ministry of Defence actually train 145 women to carry arms.[28] Thus, the articles in Canadian newspapers that suggested that Finnish women fought as soldiers were sensationalist fiction misrepresenting the activities of the Lotta Svärd.

Draft Women To Fight Reds

One of Finnish women who have been drafted for army service as ski-troops receiving one of her first skiing lessons under military instructors near Helsinki recently. The Finns have reported many successful attacks by their silently gliding ski troops in surprise attacks on the invading Russians.

During the Winter War, hundreds of Finnish-Canadian men volunteered to go to Finland where they joined the "American Legion."

Some Finnish-Canadian women, eager to heed Finland's call for help, also traveled to Finland. Their departures were covered with great fanfare. The women were depicted as hoping to join the famous Lotta Svärd organization. For example: "Mrs. Lenki Dankar [sic] is attractive, blonde and Finnish. She hopes to leave Toronto in a few days for her nativeland to serve in the front line trenches." The emphasis on the woman's looks, combined with the "fact" that she was going to serve in the "front line trenches," fortified the tantalizing image of beautiful, blonde, Finnish female warriors.[i]

Another headline declared that Mrs. Salonen, "Would sell her furniture to fight again for Finland: Twice decorated by homeland Toronto woman is anxious to return."[ii] Although "heroic and attractive" women in battle intrigued the press and offered impressions of role reversals, they were fictitious. Only eleven Finnish-Canadian women left with the volunteers to serve in some capacity during the Winter War. Three of them were accepted into the Lotta Svärd auxiliary where they worked as cooks and nurses. All three had been members of the organization before emigrating to Canada. Other immigrant women were rejected and bitterly concluded, "We weren't good enough." There were no follow-up articles on the women's experience in Finland, leaving the reader with the false impression that Finnish-Canadian women were "flocking" to serve in the front line trenches of the Winter War.[iii]

THE FUNDRAISER

While the Finnish army defends its land, relatives in Toronto are working hard to raise money and supply necessities through the Canadian Red Cross. Members of the "Finnish War Aid Auxiliary" are busily knitting and sewing at the Church of All Nations and other gathering places while they think of their beloved homeland. Funds were raised also with concerts and special performances as suggested in the photograph on the next page.

FOR THEIR BELOVED ANCESTRAL FINLAND THESE CANADIAN GIRLS SING

TONIGHT IN MASSEY HALL THE CHOIR SINGS IN AID OF FINNISH RELIEF

These are two members of the Finnish choir, which sings tonight in Massey Hall. Matti Pennanen is their conductor. Their songs of their native Finland will be an accompaniment to the travelogue film shown by Burton Holmes the lecturer, including pictures taken in Finland as late as last summer. Signe Miettinen (RIGHT) arranges the bandeau which is part of the gay costume of Sirkka Pennanen. Rt. Hon. Arthur Meighen is chairman tonight, and will give a 15-minute broadcast at 9.30. The net proceeds are being turned over to Finnish relief by the trustees of Massey Hall.

Throughout the settlement history of Finnish Canadians, women carried the main responsibility for raising funds.[32] The fundraising activity intensified just prior to the Winter War. The community issued carefully worded, short news releases designed to solicit funds for Finland while at the same time calming any fears of disloyalty to Canada, such as the following: "Following a mass meeting of Finnish people at the Church of All Nations, at which an expression of loyalty to the Canadian government was passed unanimously, an organizing meeting of captains was held." The article continued to cover all bases by describing how women planned to "do handwork during the winter for the Red Cross of Finland, should the need arise, and to assist enlisted Finnish men in the Canadian army and Canadian soldiers in general."[33] Finns soon discovered what kind of stories would make it into the media. They included interviews with worried Finnish-Canadian women with family in Finland but also pictures of Finnish-Canadian women in their national costumes. In fact, just scanning the newspapers one gets the impression that Finnish-Canadian women routinely wore this outfit. The community learned that young and beautiful women were the ones most likely to be photographed by reporters. Since the object was to raise money it was important to get photographs into the press that would draw attention to their printed message. For example, a photograph of four Finnish-Canadian women in national costumes, knitting and sewing, has the caption: "Finnish fighters supported by Toronto kin." The text below the photograph stated the community's fundraising message: "While the Finnish army defends its land, relatives in Toronto are working hard to raise money and supply necessities through the Canadian Red Cross. Here are a few members of the 'Finnish War Aid Auxiliary' busily knitting and sewing at the Church of All Nations while they think of their beloved homeland."[34] The women are then identified by name and their position in the auxiliary, except for Signe Miettinen who is identified as a "1938 Finnish beauty contest winner."

During the following months the smiling photograph of Signe Miettinen in her national costume was published many times in different poses as the photographers focused their lenses on the "beauty queen." The treasurer of the Finland Aid organization in Toronto, Elsie Kojola, who still sixty years later values her collection of newspaper clippings of the period, explained in an interview how the Finland Aid organization appointed press secretaries and staged photo opportunities in order to get their fundraising message across: "We discovered that beautiful, young women in national costumes worked the best."[35] Finnish-Canadian women were consciously part of image-building for the "Finnish Woman." The need to raise funds was paramount in their minds and the end justified the means. Thus, images of smiling costumed women proliferated the papers. The *Toronto Star* carried two more photographs of Finnish women in Toronto "who donned national costumes." The women, once again, are sewing. An adjacent picture shows piles of money scattered on the table. Smiling Mrs. Lina [*sic*] Aho is donating the funds to a Red Cross Nurse "for their campaign to give help to their homeland." Another two women packing clothes for shipment to Finland were featured the following day.[36] Images of the smiling women in traditional costumes continued to be printed regularly throughout, and even for a few months after, the Winter War.

Another image which worked well for fundraising purposes was to show women and children who were victims of war. A long-sustained fundraising campaign called "Help for Heroic Finland" in the *Montreal Star*, featured a photograph of a sad and tired looking elderly woman. Her image was designed to evoke the sympathies of Montrealers who may have been able to identify with the plight of this one woman, who reminded people of their mothers and grandmothers. The photograph and the accompanying article brought the human tragedy of Finland to the homes of Montreal:

> The tragedy that is Finland seems to peer out of the face of this elderly Finnish woman as she sits in a shelter…the face is sorrowful, but there is determination and strength written on it, as it is written all over the little Republic which is fighting for its life against overwhelming odds…Take one more glance at the pitiful, almost beseeching, face of the destitute Finnish woman pictured above, and resolve to send a donation NOW.[37]

CONCLUSION

In exploring the gendered nature of the iconography of Canadian newspapers' coverage of Finnish women in Canada during Finland's Winter War against Russia, this essay explores a little studied topic, namely the role that the media played in rallying readers to the cause of war by drawing on gendered and ethnic images of foreign women who, though not despised, were not normally seen in heroic terms. At the same time, racialized notions of beauty also mattered, and Finnish women conveniently fit with exotic – but not too exotic – notions of "white goddesses." Revealed here are the changing and mutable cultural and political meanings that were applied to a normally marginal group of immigrant women in Canada.

FOR WAR WORK—Mrs. Lina Aho and a Red Cross nurse display some of the $600 raised by local Finns in their campaign to give help to their homeland

Help For Heroic Finland

The tragedy that is Finland's seems to peer out of the face of this elderly Finnish woman as she sits in a shelter in the Swedish border town of Haparanda, where she and hundreds of women and children found refuge in their flight from Soviet bombing attacks. The face is sorrowful, but there is determination and strength written on it, as it is written all over the little Republic which is fighting for its life against overwhelming odds.

GALLANT Finland's urgent call for aid is finding a generous response in the hearts of the good people of Montreal.

The usually tranquil Finnish consular office has galvanized into busy life. A steady stream of well-wishers offering material or financial help attests to the sympathy for the plight of the Finnish people.

Norwegians, Swedes, Danes, Jews, Hungarians, English, French, and even German names are on the list of callers. Consuls of other countries, too, have rallied to the call.

News today from many parts of the civilized world brings out in bold relief the anxiety of all decent peoples to stem the tide of barbaric plunderers and the forces of primitive savagery.

France is sending military aid. Finnish volunteers are arriving in their native land from the Western Hemisphere. Supplies and money are going from the United States.

While the response has been magnificent, there is still urgent need of further funds. All lovers of human liberty will want to lighten the road of despair now being travelled by the sorely pressed Finnish people.

Take one more glance at the pitiful, almost beseeching, face of the destitute Finnish woman pictured above, and resolve to send a donation NOW

The tragedy that is Finland's seems to peer out of the face of this elderly Finnish woman as she sits in a shelter in the Swedish border town of Haparanda, where she and hundreds of women and children found refuge in their flight from Soviet bombing attacks. The face is sorrowful, but there is determination and strength written on it, as it is written all over the little Republic which is fighting for its life against overwhelming odds.

The media coverage of the Finnish women must be evaluated in its exceptional wartime context. For a few months the insatiable desire of the Canadian media to glorify the events in Finland pre-empted their critical observation skills. So distorted was the media coverage that most Canadians, and Finnish Canadians in particular, were stunned to learn that these heroes in fact lost the Winter War and ultimately, in 1940, had to make severe concessions to the Soviet Union. The headlines had described one Finnish victory after another and declared the near annihilation of the Russian army as David was defeating Goliath. Russian women and children also suffered but received no sympathy from the Canadians. Russian soldiers were brutally slaughtered by the thousands and many, unable to move with their heavy equipment, froze in the bitterly cold winter. Their slaughter was not necessarily heroic. Similarly, the images of women were designed, largely by the propaganda agencies of Finland, to create a multilayered super woman, attractive to all readers. She was at once sensual and exotic, beautiful and healthy, traditional yet modern and emancipated.

This glorification of Finland benefited, even if only briefly, the Finnish Canadians who supported Finland's war effort. For decades, the Finns had been marginalized and shunned by the media, attracting attention only when they did something that offended Canadian sensibilities. Now, suddenly, they could do no wrong. For a few months the Finnish Canadians, while distraught over the events in their homeland, basked in their hero status and tried to use it to their best advantage. Nationalistic community leaders painted a false picture of a united Finnish-Canadian community whose political differences had all but disappeared. The community learned to use its women, frequently described as "girls," to promote its nationalistic message and to aid in its fundraising. No one tried to correct or contradict the one-sided messages and often erroneous depictions of the role of Finnish women during the Winter War that had been constructed by the various propaganda agencies, the newspapers, and the Finnish-Canadian community.

The goodwill and attention towards Finland and its women was fleeting. National costumes from enemy nations soon fell out of favour. As the heroes turned into enemies, their community was silenced. No more feminine street cleaners or smiling beauty queens from Finland adorned the newspapers. Stories of Finnish women were replaced by information and intense propaganda about Canadian women's war efforts and the exotic Finnish woman vanished from the press. The mythical "Finnish Woman" had served her purpose. Her stories and images had sold newspapers, she had created goodwill and sympathy toward Finland's war effort, she had shown that women could be unified in the support of their homeland, she had provided examples of unusual working situations, her dedication in women's auxiliary work had served as a model, and she was also depicted as a soldier standing "beside the men."

The stranger became a familiar sister, a role model with whom Anglo-Canadian women could identify. Like them, she was battling cold climates, she was Protestant and white, educated, and her country needed her. This made her a well-suited warm-up act to the publicity campaigns that recruited Canadian housewives into war industries and later into the Canadian army, navy, and air force. For a fleeting moment in history the stranger had a familiar face. She was a Finnish sister peering out of Canada's major daily newspapers.

This article was first published in Sisters or Strangers? Immigrant, Ethnic, and Radicalized Women in Canadian History, *edited by Marlene Epp, Franca Iacovetta, Frances Swyripa, University of Toronto Press, Toronto, Canada, 2004, and is reprinted with permission of University of Toronto Press.*

ENDNOTES

[1] See, for example, Carmela Patrias, "Relief Strike: Immigrant Workers and the Great Depression in Crowland, Ontario, 1930–1935," and Ian Radforth, "Finnish Radicalism and Labour Activism in the Northern Ontario Woods," in Franca Iacovetta et al., eds, *A Nation of Immigrants: Women, Workers, and Communities in Canadian History, 1840s–1960s* (Toronto: University of Toronto Press, 1998), pp. 293–316, pp. 322–58.

[2] See, for example, Franca Iacovetta, Roberto Perin, and Angelo Principe, *Enemies Within: Italians and other Internees in Canada and Abroad* (Toronto: University of Toronto Press, 2000); Frances Swyripa and John Heard Thompson, eds, *Loyalties in Conflict: Ukrainians in Canada during the Great War* (Edmonton: Canadian Institute of Ukrainian Studies, 1983); Norman Hillmer, Bohdan Kordan, and Lubomyr Luciuk, eds, *On Guard for Thee: War, Ethnicity and the Canadian State, 1939–1945* (Ottawa: Canadian Committee for the History of the Second World War, 1988).

[3] See also Ken Adachi, *The Enemy That Never Was: A History of Japanese Canadians* (Toronto: McClelland and Stewart, 1976); Ann Gomer Sunahara, *The Politics of Racism: The Uprooting of Japanese Canadians during the Second World War* (Toronto: Lorimer, 1981); Barry Broadfoot, *Years of Sorrow, Years of Shame: The Story of Japanese Canadians in World War II* (Toronto: Double Day Canada, 1972); Patricia Roy, J.L. Granatstein, Masuko Ino, and Hiroko Takamura, eds, *Mutual Hostages: Canadians and Japanese during the Second World War* (Toronto: University of Toronto Press, 1990).

[4] For information on the wartime experience of Finnish Canadians, see Varpu Lindström, *From Heroes to Enemies: Finns in Canada, 1937–1947* (Beaverton, ON: Aspasia Books, 2000).

[5] J.L. Granatstein and J.M. Hitsman, *Broken Promises: A History of Conscription in Canada* (Toronto: Oxford University Press, 1977), p. 135.

[6] *Toronto Daily Star*, 2 December 1939; *Globe and Mail*, 25 December 1939; *Toronto Daily Star*, 30 December 1939; 2 January 1940, and 8 January 1940.

[7] Ministry of Foreign Affairs Archives, Finland, package 2, Finnish Consulate General of Montreal archives, *Toronto Daily Star*, 8 March 1940; *Toronto Telegram*, 11 March 1940.

[8] For example, see multipage photo essays in the *Star Weekly*, 18 November 1939 and the *Montreal Standard*, 9 December 1939.

[9] On the recruitment and image of Canadian women in the armed forces, see Ruth Roach Pierson, *"They're Still Women After All": The Second World War and Canadian Womanhood* (Toronto: McClelland and Stewart, 1986). On women and sexuality during the war, see Marilyn Lake, "Female Desires: The Meaning of World War II," in Joan Wallach Scott, ed., *Feminism in History* (Toronto: Oxford University Press, 1996), pp. 429-49.

[10] *Toronto Star*, 5 December 1939.

[11] *Star Weekly*, 16 December 1939.

[12] *Montreal Standard*, 9 December 1939.

[13] *Toronto Star*, 10 November 1939.

[14] *Montreal Standard*, 9 December 1939; *Star Weekly*, 30 December 1939.

[15] *Star Weekly*, 30 December 1939.

[16] Lea Tuiremo, *Sota ja Nainen (War and Woman)*, Snellman Institute Series B/31 (Kuopio, Finland, 1992), p. 28.

[17] *Montreal Star*, 29 December 1939; *Toronto Star*, 1 December 1939.

[18] Interview with Aune Jokinen, Sault Ste Marie, 1998. See also Lindström, *From Heroes to Enemies*, pp. 155–6.

[19] On recruitment of Canadian women into war industries, see Pierson *"They're Still Women After All."*

[20] *Montreal Standard*, 9 December 1939.

[21] Nellie McClung, "Finns Fight for Freedom against Russian Invasion: Finland Is Crowned with Immortality as Russia Attempts to Blot Out Her Independent Little Neighbor." Unidentified newspaper clipping, 20 January 1940.

[22] *Star Weekly*, 4 December 1939.

[23] *Toronto Star*, 5 December 1939.

[24] *Montreal Standard*, 9 December 1939; *Toronto Star*, 17 January 1940.

[25] *Toronto Star*, 30 November 1939.

[26] *Globe and Mail*, 1 January 1940.

[27] *Toronto Star*, 8 January 1940.

[28] Tuiremo, *Sota ja Nainen*, pp. 30–4; for a comprehensive treatment of this organization, see V. Lukkarinen, *Suomen Lotat* (Finland's Lottas) (Jyväskylä, Finland, 1986).

[29] *Toronto Star*, 2 January 1940.

[30] *Toronto Star*, 1 January 1940.

[31] University of Turku Archives SSK no. 81, letters from Anni Korsberg to Finland Society, Vaasa, 19 January 1941; Lempi Tiinus to A. Suomal. Kotiuttamisosasto, Viljakkala, 6 November 1940; Laura Virta to Päämajan Vapaaehtoistoimisto, Järvenpää, 28 October 1940; Aili Viita to Päämajan Vapaaehtoistoimisto, 14 November 1940; Interview with Helmi Huttunen, Astoria, Oregon, 1992. For further information of Finnish-Canadian women in the Winter War of Finland, see Varpu Lindström, *From Heroes to Enemies*, pp. 98–9.

[32] For a history of Finnish immigrant women in Canada, see Varpu Lindström-Best, *Defiant Sisters: A Social History of Finnish Immigrant Women in Canada, 1890–1930* (Toronto: Multicultural History Society of Ontario, 1988) — reprinted 2003 under author's name Varpu Lindström by Aspasia Books.

[33] *Toronto Star*, 10 November 1939.

[34] *Toronto Star*, 6 December 1939.

[35] Interview with Elsie Kojola, Toronto, 1998 and her private collection of newspaper clippings; York University Archives, Varpu Lindström collection.

[36] *Toronto Star*, 4 January 1940.

[37] *Montreal Star*, newspaper clipping, n.d., in Kojola collection.